Joan P.

Saints
for
Contemporary
Women

Saints
for
Contemporary
Women

Mary Hester Valentine

THE THOMAS MORE PRESS
Chicago, Illinois

ISBN 0-88347-210-4

Contents

To the saints I have loved, canonized
and uncanonized, living and dead.

St. Hilda of Whitby
614–680

W HAT does a seventh-century abbess have in common with a 20th century woman, a 20th century Catholic? The first reaction to the question will probably be: not much, if anything; and that reaction would be 100 percent wrong. We tend to believe that women today are beginning to achieve advantages never before given their sex. The fact of the matter is, if we examine the life of St. Hilda and a good many of her women contemporaries, that we are only now beginning to make the first steps backward to an eminence and acceptance that a respectable number of women in the so-called dark ages had achieved on the basis of competence.

St. Hilda, almost unknown in America today, is still admired in England as one of the most influential women of her day. The early historian, Leland, speaks of a "life of St. Hilda" by an unknown pen, which he said he saw in the library of Whitby Abbey when he visited it during the reign of Henry VIII. This volume is now, unfortunately, lost; but we do have an early life by St. Bede, long recognized as one of the most reliable of early chroniclers.

But first, it is good to go back a few centuries to understand the cultural milieu in which Hilda lived, since it was this Anglo-Saxon civilization which supported and encouraged her growth and development.

The rise and progress of civilization in the British Isles is a story shrouded in mystery. The Roman legions found the Britons strong in their fortresses and ardent in their Druidism. As early as the fourth century, however, Christianity had a strong hold in Britain. That the faith established by the Celtic missionaries was both Catholic and Roman was proved long ago by Professor Bury of Trinity college. Celts christianized the north; St. Augustine, sent by Gregory the Great, landed at Kent in the south and converted Ethelbert, who had married a Christian, Bertha, daughter of Charibert I, king of Paris.

The intellectual acumen of the Anglo-Saxon woman was recognized; the Anglo-Saxon male accorded her a unique position. Her dignity was respected, her ability was acknowledged, and her freedom was unquestioned. Among the noble thanes her education was planned with good sense, high spirituality and broad intellectual ideas. Girls learned reading and writing, the arts, domestic matters, and weaving and spinning; and those who opted for religious life were obliged to spend at least two hours daily in reading and study—a rule which presumed the ability to do what was required.

Abbesses were in such great esteem for their learning, sanctity and prudence that they were summoned to Councils; and their names follow those of bishops and precede those of priests and lesser clerics in the signatures on documents.

It was into this environment that St. Hilda was born, the daughter of Hereric, nephew to King Edwin. In her early youth she was baptized with her uncle, the king, by the Roman missionary Paulinus, which fact did not prevent her from leaning to the side of the Celtic missionaries. For the first 33 years of her life she lived in the courts in what must be acknowledged as a cultured situation.

Since the excavations at Sutton Hoo, above the estuary of the Deben, it is no longer possible to regard the culture of the Anglo-Saxon courts as a stunted and poverty-stricken version of the environment which surrounded the barbarian kings of larger peoples. The undisturbed burialship has yielded materials which throw the whole history of that period into a new perspective. The ship with its wealth was buried certainly in the first half and probably in the first quarter of the seventh century, while Hilda was still living.

Many of the articles are of a kind commonly, or at least occasionally, associated with other rich burials of this age: sword and sheath, shield, helmet, spear-heads, bronze bowls of more than one type, buckets ornamented with decorative metal work, horns with silver mounts. The notable feature of these objects is the remarkable elaboration of their adornment. There is a portable flambeau, a five stringed musical instrument, a purse with a golden frame containing forty gold coins, and a leather bag with silver handles. The outstanding feature of the discovery is the large number of objects in various metals, and few treasures at all comparable have been found in any part of the whole Germanic north. Apart from their intrinsic value, which is very great, the gold objects were made with technical excellence and unusual decorations. They are undoubtedly of English workmanship, and as pieces of design they are unmatched.

The silver objects comprise a large dish, a fluted bowl, and a nest of nine small bowls which when dug up were so exactly matched that only the top and bottom dish were tarnished. There was also a lovely silver ladle. All of this is a prized exhibit in the British Museum in London.

None of this would have any purpose in a biography of Hilda were it not to indicate that, brought up as she was in court, she was familiar with similar objects; and historians have under-estimated, or at least under-stressed, the wealth and sophistication of a great 7th-century English king.

Of course, those who have read Beowulf, that early Anglo-Saxon epic, will remember the queen Wealhtheow who "walked in state," among her guests, and presented the glittering loving cup to Beowulf

> "with courteous bow
> greeting him graciously,
> giving him bracelets of twisted gold,
> a robe and rings, and the rarest collar,"

after which she asked him to "instruct my boys in gentle manners." Not a barbaric request.

When Hilda was thirty-three she felt a call to leave the court and enter religious life. She planned to give

St. Hilda of Whitby

God her life, leave family, world and country and enter the monastery in Celles, France. Saint Aiden, Bishop of Northumbria, convinced her that her work for God was in England. He then gave her lands by the River Wear, and there she spent a year in prayer and good works with a few companions in preparation. In the meantime the abbess of nearby Hartlepool retired, and Aiden appointed Hilda superior of the monastery. Probably her predecessor had not been a successful leader, for St. Bede noted in his *Ecclesiastical History* that one of the first things done by Hilda was to introduce order into the monastery.

Nine years later, in 657, St. Hilda was given land by King Oswy to establish a new monastery at Whitby, so called because of the white cliffs on which the monastery was built in the North Riding of Yorkshire. The ruins, even today, are impressive, and give some indication of the vast size of the establishment and the complex work done there. "Of all the sites chosen by monastic architects, after that of Monte Cassino," says Montalembert, "I know none grander and more picturesque than that of Whitby."

What was unusual from a 20th-century point of view is that Whitby was a double monastery, with the one for men existing side by side with that for women. Even more striking is the fact that when the two groups met to elect their leader they chose the most obvious and best administrator, St. Hilda. Double monasteries were an economic convenience, the efficiency of which was often due to the fact that both were supervised by a woman. In fact, it is doubtful whether at this time there were any houses founded only for women in England, although some, as at Whitby, had cells or minor convents subordinate to the main monastery. The one attached to Whitby was at Hackness, a lovely valley enclosed by foliaged hills, to which St. Hilda frequently retreated in old age for meditation and prayer, and to escape from the constant demands on her time from visitors who came to her for counsel, often enough on trivial matters.

But for many years before that happy time, her life was dedicated to the well-being not only of those religious in her double monastery, but also to the larger monastic family—the people who worked for the abbey, or formed the nucleus of the future town or city. The monastic church was the scene, not only of the liturgy of the monks and nuns, but also of the services for the laity of the district.

Apparently the dark ages were more enlightened than our own. I can not visualize a group of monks today electing as their superior the head of a nearby convent, even if they both lived by the same Rule. Catholic men's and women's colleges which have emerged in the 20th century rarely have women presidents. I say "rarely" as a safeguard; at the moment I cannot think of any. Columbia University recently publicized the election of its first woman academic dean.

But back in the 7th-century St. Hilda personally supervised the erection of both the church and monastery. Bede says, "Great was her pleasure to see a fabric rising and advancing regularly, in which she was to spend the remainder of her days, where she could enjoy her native air, live retired from the world, and be instrumental toward the salvation of her neighbors."

Her community reached vast proportions. Her spiritual sway extended over hundreds of souls in both the nunnery and the monastery, and obviously her keen sense of justice was probably the characteristic which caused her to give such perfect satisfaction as an executive. Special stress should also be laid on her prudence, since this virtue drew crowds to Whitby to consult her, ordinary folk as well as the nobility. The strictness with which the rules were observed can be inferred from the good repute of her monastery.

Leibell says that her double monastery for more than thirty years was a model of order, union, charity and equality, so much so that it became usual to point it out as an image of the primitive church, which had neither rich nor poor, and where all was common among Christians.

St. Hilda inspired the monks under the monastery's rule with so great a devotion, so true a love of the Scriptures and such careful study of them, that her monastery became a school of missionaries and bishops. Interesting is the human note given by Bede, that she would not permit her scholars to stay up too long, for she maintained that the mind is keener for study after sleep.

The work done in Whitby under her guidance was of a high spiritual and intellectual character, and the monastery yielded five bishops to the Saxon Church— men of singular merit and sanctity, according to Bede. Bede himself was indebted to the influence of the efficient abbess, for he was a disciple of St. John of Beverly, one of the five bishops from the Whitby abbey. Bede exemplifies the sacred and secular lore acquired in Whitby, and is recognized as the first English historian to "check his sources."

Fuller calls Hilda the most learned woman before the Conquest and names her the "female Gamaliel at whose feet many learned men had their education."

But St. Hilda is remembered today, by those few who recall her at all, as the mother of English literature. Whitby was an important center of culture where books were prized, stored and multiplied. Nuns as well as monks were busy transcribing manuscripts, making their own parchment, ink and pigment. It was a gathering place on feast days not only for the monks and nuns and their students, but also for the larger monastic family outside the walls—farmers, herdsmen, tanners, metal workers—and after the special meal of celebration, entertainment which Hilda had experienced in the great hall of her uncle was adapted to the local audience.

Students of the fragments of Anglo-Saxon literature which have survived agree that this was not literature in the making, but a highly sophisticated poetry with structured rules of prosody: a strongly rhythmic four-beat line (when the line has only three beats it is obvious the minstrel supplied the fourth with a stroke of his harp), alliteration with its own rules for stressed and unstressed syllables, a unique use of metaphor, and repetition to help the memory of the minstrel. In our century Ezra Pound, Wilbur and T. S. Eliot have imitated it in several poems; and Gerard Manley Hopkins,

16

the first of contemporary poets, was fascinated by its possibilities. The poetry was so familiar that it was customary for the audience to join in the chanted recitative; and as the musician became tired it was not unusual for him to pass the harp to a companion sitting next to him, who would take up the sung tale where it had been left off.

Since Whitby was home to educated men and women it is clear that the custom of passing the harp at these festivities was an ordinary occurrence.

Bede, again, is our authority for the story of Caedmon, but we can fill in imaginatively the setting for the birth of the first English poem. One evening after the high feast day meal, when the servants of the monastery were gathered about the table with the monks and nuns for good fellowship, the harp was passed from hand to hand. Among those present was the middle-aged cowherd, Caedmon, uneducated and embarrassed at these gatherings. As he knew nothing of poetry, when he saw the harp approaching him he slipped away from the company in shame, retiring to the cattle shed where he was assigned for the night to care for the draught cattle. As he slept a voice called him by name and said, "Sing me something."

"I can not sing," Caedmon answered. "That is why I left the supper."

The voice repeated, "Sing, notwithstanding."

"What shall I sing?" asked Caedmon.

"Sing the beginning of the world, the creation." At once he began to sing the sacred story, and, upon awakening, he remembered the words and repeated them to his neighbors.

St. Hilda was told of the strange happening. She sent for the new poet, and questioned him in the presence of the learned in her monastery. Through her "the clumsy cowherd from whose lips flowed the first great English song" found sympathy and encouragement. With a woman's intuition she detected more than ordinary genius in him, and accepted him as a special gift from God to the monastery. She had him taught the Scriptures, educated him for the priesthood, and gave him every opportunity to cultivate his talent.

One need not naively believe that Caedmon was taught by an angel. Simply by being present in the hall during the long winter evenings, listening to the minstrels chant the old familiar tales, he had served an apprenticeship which he himself did not know. That he had absorbed some of the intellectual discussions in the monastery is obvious, and that he had untapped poetic talent is clear. Robert Burns was also humble in birth and a farm hand; and Walt Whitman, recognized as one of America's great poets, stopped his formal education after the sixth grade. The important point of the story of Caedmon is that Hilda's recognition of his gift and her education of the man indicate a woman of large heart and broad mind. Without her penetrating insight into his potential, her indifference to social class differences, our language and literature would be poorer.

Bede reflects, "She embraced the grace of God in the man, associated him with the rest of the brethren, and ordered that he should be taught the whole series of sacred history. Thus Caedmon, keeping in mind all he heard . . . converted the same into most harmonious

verse; and sweetly repeating the same, made his masters in their turn his hearers."

There is no doubt that this newly discovered poet
found favor on feast days and helped to satisfy the
narrative desires of the monastic inhabitants, and one
can imagine Hilda's gratification as she sat in her abba-
tial chair and listened to what her wisdom had helped
develop.

But all was not sweetness and light in ecclesiastical
England of that day. The problem, like many which
plague the church since Vatican II, was not a problem
of dogma but basically a liturgical one. Father Broderick, elaborating on Bede's account, points out that the
difficulty was that of Celtic vs. Roman customs, especially the problem of Easter. Broderick notes that the
paschal controversy was a question rather of mathematics and astronomy than of religion. In Northumbria, according to Bede, Celtic traditions were followed. Consequently King Oswy and his household
were celebrating Easter while his queen, who followed
the Roman system of the south, was still fasting.

Actually the Celts had not invented their own
system; it was simply that in vogue when their
churches were first organized. It was the old Roman
method; to give it up was to cast a slur upon their
origin. Rome itself, and the rest of the Western church,
had given up the old method and adopted not one but
several revised systems of calculating the calendar. But
the Celts were isolated, and their conservatism really
made them more Roman than the Romans. (Does it
sound a contemporary note?) Actually, of course, there
were no decrees of the Apostolic See at that time,

except that Easter must be kept on a Sunday; the New Testament, obviously, has nothing to say on the subject.

But the division cut deep into the fabric of Catholicism. Whether its solution was due to Hilda or not we do not know; but it was her monastery that was the scene of the healing, and certainly her influence was one of the decisive factors in securing unity in the English churches. The famous Council of Whitby was called in 664 when Hilda was fifty years old. To it came King Oswy with bishops Colman and Chad to represent the Celtic customs handed down to them by St. Aiden. What a scene it must have been with the king on one side, and the smiling queen, her ladies, other churchmen, and the pugnacious Wilfrid on the other. And Hilda, who together with her community clung to the Celtic tradition, quietly willing to accept either decision so that peace might prevail.

King Oswy opened the proceedings with a little exhortation on the need for unity of practice among those who were serving the same God and seeking the same kingdom of Heaven. Let them, he urged, investigate which was the true rule for determining the date of Easter, and let all adhere to that.

St. Colman said, "The Easter rule I follow I received from my forefathers who sent me here as bishop. We read that the blessed Evangelist John . . . observed it, together with all the churches under his care."

Wilfrid advocated the adoption of the Roman cycle, stating a powerful apocryphal and unanswerable case: "The Easter which I observe is that which I myself have seen celebrated in Rome where the blessed apostles Peter and Paul lived, preached, suffered and are buried." Wilfrid, of course, as Father Broderick points out, was magnificently anachronistic. He had only to read St. Augustine's 23rd letter to learn that in 387 Gaul kept Easter on March 21, Italy on April 18, and Egypt on April 25.

But there was no one at the Whitby Council to contradict Wilfrid; and King Oswy, determined not to offend St. Peter, declared that he "dare no longer contradict the decrees of him who keeps the doors of the Kingdom of Heaven, lest he should refuse me admission."

And so at Whitby, under the watchful eyes of St. Hilda, was settled not only the question of the paschal cycle, but also whether the church in England should link her fortunes with those of the declining and loosely compacted Irish church or with the rising power and organization of Rome.

For Hilda it was a decisive about-face. Although she and her double community had professed and favored the Celtic rule and observance, they gave them up after the Council of Whitby. Also at this council the Rule of St. Benedict was definitively adopted for all monasteries in England; and a whole new rule of life became that of the double monastery, with Hilda still director and leader.

Shortly after the council Hilda became ill with a fever which weakened her for a period of six years, during which, Bede tells us, "she never failed to return thanks to her Maker, and publicly and privately instructed those committed to her charge, for by her own example she admonished all to serve God in perfect health and to return him thanks in adversity or bodily infirmity." The illness reached a crisis on November 17, 680, when she called together the servants of God in the monastery, admonishing them to preserve evangelical peace among themselves. Her dying advice to those gathered around her was, "Love one another; it is the Christian virtue."

She had given of her warm affection during her long life, and could expect to be listened to when she gave the same advice to others. Bede, so reserved in his expression, is extravagant when speaking of Hilda. We get what we give in life. No character unloving or unlovable could arouse such affection in her subjects as did Mother Hilda, the first abbess of Whitby. Her contemporaries dwell on her amiable traits, and even the 20th-century biographer, David Hugh Farmer, in 1978 felt impelled to slip in a contemporary editorial comment: She was an excellent example of how in the Anglo-Saxon church an able woman could achieve great influence and authority.

Julian of Norwich
1342-1416

A MERICAN Catholics tend to be a pragmatic group; their prayer life is patterned and methodical. While Carmelite nuns were among the first to settle in the United States, and the contemplative life has always attracted some, their number has been comparatively small. Mysticism and contemplation for many years were considered gifts restricted to the few. Attendance at Sunday Mass; a certain amount of mortification, chiefly during Lent; avoidance of sin; and regularity in prayer were the heights to which most Catholics aspired. Union with God was an ideal, of course; but "real" union could only be achieved by experiencing the beatific vision—and that could happen only after death. Most people did not know any real live mystics, or thought they did not (the fact of the matter is, probably most of us do know one or more; for the real contemplative, one who experiences the immediacy of God in his daily life and speaks to him with the casualness of the hero of "Fiddler on the Roof," does not advertise the fact.)

What the majority of American Catholics twenty-five or more years ago forgot was that they had been taught contemplation, or interior prayer, when they were very small; and it is doubtful that the effect of that early teaching has ever left them. Those preparing children for First Communion have always made it clear that the time after the reception of the Eucharist was a very special time—a time to talk to Jesus as intimately as one would to a friend. There is a beautiful story of a child who reported that she had recited her multiplication tables for Jesus because the fact that she had mastered them had so delighted her parents the evening before that she was sure it would make Jesus happy, too. But most of us forget that talking to God is a special gift of the spirit, and when we do talk with him we are particularly blessed.

But mystics? Mystical prayer? Not for Americans. Andrew Greeley pointed out in *Ecstasy, A Way of Knowing* in 1974 that "As recently as a decade ago a mystical experience would probably have been treated by most intelligent people who heard about it as a form of mental illness. . . . If any mystics remained in the Catholic Church, they kept it a deep, dark secret, because clearly a mystic would not be a very effective second-grade teacher or assistant pastor."

That has changed, as young people in the 60's became disenchanted with the materialism they saw about them, the lack of motivation for anything except on a personal, acquisitive level. The Korean and Vietnam wars introduced many to Zen Buddhism, to Hindu "holy men," and to levels of quiet contemplation that they had not experienced in their Western prayer life; and they were intrigued. There were charlatans among the leaders, of course, who betrayed the trust of

24

the innocent and naive: gurus who formed cults in which disciples found a community they had not known before, and under the influence of drug-induced euphoria, were encouraged to behave erratically and to beg on the streets, enriching the leaders' coffers.

Granted that some of that so-called mysticism was spurious, we are still forced to acknowledge a growing and authentic interest in Christian mystics and an increase in books about the great Catholic mystics, as well as a muted acknowledgment on the part of many Catholics that they themselves have had spiritual experiences that took them out of themselves. McCready and Greeley's study, carried out at NORC, produced evidence that about half the Americans polled reported having had spiritual experiences they could not explain; and about a fifth acknowledged these to be frequent. Merton's writings became popular, and Dag Hammarskjold's *Markings* a best seller.

It was inevitable, given this climate, that some of the great mystics of the 14th century should be reprinted, studied, and given critical analysis by theologians; and that they should slowly but steadily slip into the popular market.

One whose work has continued to attract is Julian of Norwich, an anchoress who enjoyed popular esteem in her own lifetime for her wise counsel in spiritual matters. Her *Revelations of Divine Love,* or, as she herself called the manuscript, "The Shewings," never completely faded out of the consciousness of English Catholics. As far back as the middle 60's and early 70's of the 19th century, Julian was occasionally reprinted. But it was chiefly literary scholars of Middle English, or contemplative monks and nuns, who studied her work for obviously different reasons. Then, with the revival of interest in mystical writings in our century, both critical and popular editions of her one book have multiplied. In today's mail I received a publisher's catalog listing a new paperback edition of Julian.

I first became acquainted with Julian in a course in Middle English in which the textbook, compiled by the medieval scholar, Loomis, included some significant chapters from Dame Julian's work. She impressed me then, as she has impressed thousands, by her transparent sincerity, the theological accuracy of her words, and her clear description of an incommunicable experience. What struck me then, as I read the snippets in our textbook, and does still, was that she was not a visionary who enjoyed raptures, but a responsible, serious woman whose only desire was to love God better. She had experienced his love, and urgently desired to proclaim it to all men, so that they, too, might experience the strength and comfort it had provided her.

As Greeley noted in his study of ecstasy, Julian's life and writing exemplify the elements which constitute a true religious experience: an overwhelming feeling of being at one with God or Christ, a sense of being in the presence of God, and a deep feeling of being personally loved by Christ here and now.

Julian believed in her vision, and acknowledged that such an experience was a help; but she was quite willing to admit that if it produced no effects in the recipient's life, it might well not be authentic. God's will, as she repeatedly insists in her book, is the norm for all

Blessed Julian of Norwich

Christian living; and as Father Molinari, her first serious 20th century critic, points out, it is this complete submission to God which is the surest guarantee of her freedom from illusion and delusion. It is her ability to distinguish between what was revealed to her in that one mystical experience and what God clarified to her over the years as she prayed over and pondered what she had been shown, that makes her a singularly attractive spiritual guide for us today, even though her way of life was unique even in her own day and is nonexistent in ours.

Julian was an anchoress, that is, a solitary, living in a cell of two or three rooms built adjacent to a church (in many cases using the church for its fourth wall), devoting her life to prayer, to counseling others, and to contemplation.

There is no doubt that she is a historical character, but we know singularly little about her life, apart from what she chooses to tell us and what can be deduced from the evidence furnished in her book. We know from the *Book of Margery Kempe,* whose author visited her probably between 1400 and 1410, that she had a considerable reputation as an advisor in spiritual matters. Internal evidence shows that she was 30 years old in May, 1373; that is, she was born toward the end of 1342. She was still alive in 1416. There are references to Julian in three wills dated 1404, 1415, and 1416; and these establish that her anchorhold was at St. Julian's church, Norwich, where she lived with a companion and a cat permitted her by the *Ancren Riwle—* to take care of the mice, one supposes.

It is almost impossible to know whether or not she

was a Benedictine nun before she became an anchoress, but the fact that the Church of St. Julian belonged to the Benedictine monastery at Carrow seems to suggest she was a member of that community. She might even have been there as a girl, for the nuns had a boarding school. Certainly she had learned to read and write; she knew Latin. She does state that when she received her revelations she lacked literary skills; but these she mastered later, and became so competent that she has been compared with Chaucer for her easy use of the vernacular.

But specific details of her life before the great experience of the revelations which were to influence the rest of her life are lacking. Previously she had been an exceptionally devout woman, and there is some slight evidence that at the time she was still living at home with her mother, to whom she was devoted. She states that at some unspecified time previously she had asked God for three favors. The first was "bodily sight" of the Passion of Christ, so that she might share his sufferings in love as did his mother. The second was to have "bodily sickness, so that by suffering the physical, mental, and spiritual pains of imminent death" she might be purified in mind and heart from all love of earthly things. The third was for sorrow for sin, for suffering with Christ, and longing for God. She tells us the first two favors she asked on condition that God willed it; but she asked for the third with no conditions, for, as she says, "to have these is to be a Christian."

Her desires were granted. She became critically ill with a sickness which lasted a week, so severe that

those who watched her, including a priest, anticipated her death. It was during this period that she was granted the revelations, visions which succeeded one another and took a considerable time, in which she was granted an awareness of the suffering of Christ and of his love of humanity.

There were sixteen revelations during this week, and then no more; but she spent twenty years pondering their meaning during her hours of prayer, eventually writing down both what she had been shown and the enlightenment she had received about them "through the same Spirit that showed them." She wrote her little book, and at the end of her life revised and amended it to include whatever additional insights had come to her over the years. According to the prologue she did so because "This vision was shown for all men and not for me alone."

What is it in the book which so appeals to contemporary readers? The manager of our college book store told me that a year or so ago she could not keep copies in stock, although it is not required reading in any course nor is it suggested supplementary reading. Perhaps the reason lies in the fact that Julian lived in a period very similar to ours, a time of doubt and struggle, of confusion, war and disaster. Even Julian in her anchorhold was aware of the problem of evil, the suffering of the innocent, the despair of the destitute. Her visions had brought her close enough to God so that she, like Job, did not hesitate to question him; and to her, as to Job, came the answers. Since her responses were from the God of love of the New Testament, they differ dramatically from the answers given to Job.

Reading what she writes and letting it rest in the mind gives the seeker today something of the comfort Julian herself experienced in the recognition that our God is a "courteous, loving Lord."

It is simple enough to summarize what the book contains: the succession of bright, clear images of Our Lord crowned with thorns; Our Lady, still a girl, holding her son; and subsequent pictures. She touches on all the main issues of faith: creation, man, nature, life, grace, sin, Mary, the church. But her primary focus is on the three great mysteries: God, man, and their reconciliation. There are thousands of books which cover these topics; but none, I think, that does so with the personal, heart-warming effectiveness of Julian's. She relates everything to a single central reality: God is love, and his love overflows to all his creatures.

I shall, then, select some of the more significant statements which have relevance for us. I hope that those who have not read her will be tempted to do so, for her book has been called by Chambers "the tenderest and most beautiful exposition in the English language of God's loving dealings with man."

On one occasion when she thought of the world's grief and danger, and wondered what would become of it all, she tells us, "He showed me a little thing the size of a hazel nut, lying in the palm of my hand, and it was as round as a ball. I looked thereupon with the eye of my understanding and thought, 'What may this be?' And it was explained in general thus: 'It is the whole creation.' I marveled how it could last, for methought it might suddenly have fallen to nought for littleness.

And I was answered in my understanding. 'It lasteth, and ever shall, because God loveth it. . . . God made it, God loveth it, God keepeth it.'"

She wondered also, as many of us do, why by the foreseeing wisdom of God the beginning of sin was not prevented, "for then methought all would have been well." But Jesus answered her, "Sin is behovable; but all shall be well, and all shall be well, and all manner of things shall be well." When she persisted and asked how so much evil could be balanced, Christ reminded her that all evil flowed from the first sin; and since his passion blotted out the effects of that sin, "If I have cured the greater, can I not cure the less?"

Then Jesus said, "'Art thou well satisfied that I suffered for thee?' I said, 'Yea, good Lord.' . . . Then said our good Lord, 'If thou art satisfied, I am satisfied; for if I could suffer more I would, for the great love I bear thee.'"

He explained prayer saying, "I am the Ground of thy beseeching. First it is My will that thou have it; after that I make thee to will it; and after that, I make thee to beseech it; and thou beseechest it. How could it be, then, that thou shouldst not have thy beseeching?" The reader is reminded here that all liturgical prayers end "through Jesus Christ, Our Lord," as witness that the prayer wills what God wills.

She reminds us that Christ did not say we would not be tempted, nor be in trouble and distress; but he said, "Thou shalt not be overcome."

Her admiration for God's goodness in one section focuses on the miracle of the human body. "As the body is clad in the cloth, and the flesh in the skin, and the bones in the flesh, and the heart in the breast, so are we, soul and body, clad in the goodness of God and enclosed. Yea, and more plainly—all these may waste and wear away, but the goodness of God is ever whole." She is impressed with the skill which ordained how the body should be delivered of its waste: "A man walks upright, and the food in his body is shut in as if in a well-made purse. When the time of his necessity comes, the purse is opened, and then shut again, in most seemly fashion. And it is God who does this, as it is shown when he says that he comes down to us in our humblest needs. For he does not disdain to serve us in the simplest natural functions of our body for the love of the soul which he created in his own likeness."

"Homely" is one of her favorite words; in her day the word meant comfortable, to be at ease. Commenting on our relationship with God she says, "Our courteous Lord willeth that we should be as homely with him as heart may think or soul desire. But let us beware that we take not this homeliness so recklessly as to leave courtesy."

She is one of the first to see God and Christ as both mother and father; and she is recklessly inconsistent in her use of the terms, matching the word to the gift, a contribution certainly in tune with certain trends in contemporary theology. "As verily as God is our father, so verily is God our mother. . . . In his marvellous deep charity and foreseeing counsel of all the Trinity, he willed that the second person should become our mother. . . . In the taking of our nature he quickened us; in his blessed dying upon the cross he bore us to endless life. And from that time, and now and evermore until doomsday, he feedeth and furthereth us."

What she is trying to say, of course, is that God can not be trapped by words; and as Edmund Colledge points out, what she develops is not the idea of femininity as opposed to or distinct from that of masculinity, but that of the motherhood of God as complement to that of his fatherhood. She does not introduce in her approach to God the vocabulary and the symbolism of sex. In no way does she wish to substitute the idea of motherhood of God for that of his fatherhood; she wants simply to unite them.

She points out with clarity and precision that, in the sight of God, all men are one man, and one man is all men. She shares with us her understanding that there is no wrath in God, but only endless goodness and friendship. She had difficulty in balancing this with "one point of our faith, which is that many creatures shall be damned. . . . This being so, methought, it was impossible that all manner of things shall be well." And she says regarding this problem she had no special revelation but this: "That which is impossible to thee is not impossible to me. I shall save my word in all things, and I shall make all things well." How it shall be done, she points out, no one knows, "nor shall know till it is done. . . . Then we shall all admit without question, Lord, blessed mayest thou be, for it is thus; it is well. The greatest deeds have been done."

It is a case of seeing God in a point, that is, that he is in all things, or as Julian expresses it, "Our Lord said,

'See I am God, see! I am in all things, see! I do all things; see I never lift my hands off my works nor ever shall, without end.'"

The depth of her thought can only be grasped by a careful reading of the whole. The danger for the superficial reader lies in the fact that the profundity of her book is clothed in such simplicity that its hidden value may be overlooked, and the reader not be aware of how extraordinary both it and she are.

Franklin Chambers notes that because she was a cloistered recluse some may wonder what relevance she has for today's world, since it would seem to have restricted her outlook. And yet it was said of her that at times, "The four walls of her narrow home seem to be rent and torn asunder, and not only England, but Christendom appears before her view." Many in this last quarter of the 20th century who have read her, and found in her the answer to many of their questions, may feel that she not only saw all of Christendom, but her vision pierced down the years to enlighten "even Christians" 500 years later, as she noted that she was taught "out of God's courteous love and his endless goodness to the comfort of us all."

Catherine of Siena
1347–1380

FOREIGNERS who visit Rome are frequently puzzled by the beautiful statue of Saint Catherine of Siena on one of the most important and busy streets of the ancient city, Via della Conciliazione. If they visit the ancient church of Santa Maria sopra Minerva, the church dedicated to Our Lady built over a temple to Minerva, they will again be struck by a contemporary statue by the artist Enzo Assenza at the entrance, beckoning to worship, and within the church the sepulchre of the saint. In Siena this would be no surprise, but why in Rome? The answer a native will give is that Rome has a long memory, and the city recalls with gratitude even today that it was this young saint who persuaded the pope to leave Avignon, where he and his court had been from 1309–1377. About 40 years before her birth, the popes, aware of the anarchic state of the Empire, had fallen for the temptation of putting themselves under the rising power of France and had settled in Avignon.

Catherine's reasons for urging the return of the papacy to Rome were purely spiritual, it is true; but were it not for her success in bringing it about the city might well have become a tourist center of monuments and memories, as Corinth is today.

The historian of the popes, Pastor, considers her "one of the most marvelous figures in the history of the world; certainly one of the great women of world history." Apart from her important place in the story of a curious and violent age, in some respects surprisingly like our own, Catherine happens to be a saint—a great saint, and in many ways a puzzling one. She is one of only two women the church has honored with the title "Doctor of the Church," the other being St. Teresa of Avila, like Catherine a woman theologically uneducated but inspired to a remarkable degree by the Holy Spirit. Catherine's writings, both the letters and the famous ascetical work called *Dialogue*, are orthodox, and in spite of their somewhat florid style, challenging and inspirational reading even today.

Catherine was born in 1347, the youngest of the 25 children of Giacomo Benincasa, a dyer, and his wife, Lapa. It was a family of politically and economically independent artisans. Giacomo was a workingman who owned a good-sized house, and he could (and did on occasion) feed forty people under his own roof. His wife, Lapa, does not come off very well at the hands of biographers. She is presented as a short-tempered woman, cross and sharp-tongued. But as Phyllis McGinley notes, having to cope with 25 lively children, as well as a disobedient mystic, seems to be excuse for a hard word now and then.

Catherine had revelations even when she was a child. Returning home one day when she was six years old with her brother Stephen, who was about seven or eight, from visiting her married sister, Bonaventura, Catherine looked up and saw across the valley, above the top of the Church of the Dominicans, a royal throne. On it sat Jesus, crowned with the papal tiara and pontifical robes. Beside him stood the princes of the apostles, Peter and Paul, and St. John the Evangelist. Catherine did what any child would do: she stood still and stared at Christ, who smiled at her and blessed her as she had seen the bishop do. So powerful was the vision that she stood immobile on the road while traffic of men and animals surged around her. Her brother, who had gone on, turned and ran back in alarm, seizing her by the arm. Catherine seemed to awaken, and said with a forlorn little smile, "If you could see what I have seen, you wouldn't bother me."

The story was first told by Raymond della Vigne, an important Dominican theologian who later became Master General of the Order, not a man likely to be impressed by childish tales of visions. But whatever the explanation or authenticity of this particular first wonder in a life of wonders, it marked a decisive change in the child. From then on she followed her own path and began to carve her own career. It was some time, however, before anyone in that crowded home noticed that something had happened to Catherine. Then her mother observed that the child who had been naturally cheerful had become quiet and withdrawn, often slipping away to a nearby chapel.

As she matured she became lovely and attractive, with golden hair which was most unusual and admired in Siena then as it is today. Her mother's natural ambition was that Catherine should make a good marriage; she could not for the life of her understand why her daughter should be plagued with extravagant holiness. From early adolescence Catherine had to listen to the constant talk about when a husband would be chosen for her.

At first she did not pay a great deal of attention. She was absorbed with her own thoughts, and the urging of her heart to do something special for God. She began to get up early in the morning, before the family awoke, to pray, at first for those she knew and loved, then gradually for Italy, the suffering, and the world. At table she began to eat less and less, refusing meat entirely; and when it was put on her plate by her concerned father she would slip it to the cats under the table. And then came the announcement that shook the family's complaisance: "I will never marry; I want to keep a single heart for God." It was clear to her astonished family that she meant it. Her father suggested that they consult a relative who might find a suitable convent where the girl could have her wish, but Catherine objected. She did not want to be a nun. There were other ways to serve God, and she was certain they would be revealed to her.

Her mother, Lapa, was as determined as her daughter; and she nagged her continually until one day in a gesture of defiance Catherine cut off all her beautiful hair. Lapa then tried another tactic on what she saw as simple adolescent stubbornness: she set her doing the hardest work of the house, deprived her of her bedroom where she could pray in solitude, and forced her to wait on the rest of the family like a servant. Catherine, however, simply did as she was told with such grace and love that in frustration her parents finally gave way and allowed her to live the life she had chosen.

She had a little cell of her own where, like an athlete, she prepared for a contest by prayer and mortification. But even in things of the spirit Catherine was a prodigy, and long before she was twenty she left her cell to begin a mission to the world. It was about this time that she experienced her second mystical experience, one which was to set her on the path from which she would never turn. On Shrove Tuesday, while the city of Siena was celebrating carnival, Catherine saw Christ surrounded by Our Lady, St. John, St. Paul, and St. Dominic. Our Lady took Catherine's right hand and asked her Son to espouse her to himself. Our Lord then gave her a ring and said, "I espouse you to myself in the faith which, until you celebrate your eternal nuptuals with me in heaven you will preserve ever without stain." Ever after this, whenever Catherine looked at her finger she saw the ring.

On that day Catherine felt herself confirmed in her vocation, and felt a strong confirmation of the kind of work which she knew to be in her character: active work which would evoke a great deal of criticism.

One night she had a dream of amazing vividness in which St. Dominic held out to her the habit of his order. When she awoke she took it for a sign, and after some difficulty, because of her youth, she joined the Mantellates, the Third Order of St. Dominic in 1364.

Its vows of service and purity of life did not involve joining the cloister or leaving her home; her ministry was to be accomplished in the world, not apart from it.

At first she went into hospitals and houses of the poor. The plague swept Italy, and she nursed the sick with the same single-mindedness she had expended on her prayers. The sweetness of her nature and the success of her work so endeared her to the people of Siena that in a year or two she had become the center of a group of notable disciples. This fellowship, called the Caterinati, consisted of "old and young, priests and laymen, poets and politicians," most of whom she had rescued from lives of illness, idleness, or vice. One of these was the artist Andrew Vanni, who painted the portrait we still have of her. Another was Neri de Landoccio, the poet. The rest followed a dozen different professions. They were united only as followers of this girl whom they affectionately called "Mamma," although she was younger than any of them.

In the hospital of Santa Maria della Scala, in the vast, vaulted room where the sick lay close together, Catherine and her company worked hour after hour. She learned about suffering there, and also began to cut down her food to the point where it consisted only of water and vegetables. Likewise, and, as she admitted, with greater difficulty—she cut down on her sleep so that she would have time for prayer and counsel in her work-filled days.

This all might well have resulted in a fanatical, demanding person, unattractive socially and demanding of others. This was not so, however; the unattractive elements of her life softened her character and made her a warm, intensely sensitive woman who drew even those who opposed her initially to follow her lead. Unhappy married couples, grieving widows, puzzled mothers, sufferers of all kinds sought her out for her counsel and her comfort. Malavolti declared that Catherine was the only free woman of Italy; she came and went exactly as she pleased.

The intellectual quality of her mind was strong, clear, logical and sane. Her writing is beautiful, and Italian critics rank it with Boccaccio as the foremost exemplar of the use of the vernacular in 14th century writing. Actually, Catherine never learned to write, but dictated both her letters and the remarkable theological treatises which even today attract readers. Sometimes, like Caesar, she used three secretaries simultaneously. Obviously this profundity of insight into theology and the spiritual life can only be explained in the light of her mystical prayer, the secrets of which she revealed to no one.

Her advice to her followers was to concretize their prayer in action. "You must pray the prayer of action, which is the fragrant flower of the soul. A good man is a prayer," she said. She herself set the example, and she had a capacity for successful worldly business which was almost political, we would say today.

This was the period of unrest between the Italian city states, and also the time of conflict between the Guelphs and the Ghibellines. Siena, a mercantile city, was involved in the continuing battles; and frequently her citizens were trapped in allegiance. Even families were divided.

One of the more famous stories concerning Cather-

ine is commemorated in the statue on Via della Conciliazione in Rome. The story involves a young noble-
man, Nicholas Toldo, who was condemned to death,
apparently for somewhat frivolous political reasons.
He was storming and raging in his cell, and absolutely
refused to meet his fate either in a Christian or in a
stoical spirit. Catherine went to visit him; he was so
comforted and consoled that he went to confession and
prepared for death. He made her promise to go with
him when the time came for the execution. She promised, and fulfilled that promise. She herself tells us
what happened. "He said, 'Stay with me; do not
abandon me. Then I shall be all right; I shall die
content.' He came like a meek lamb. When he saw me
he laughed and asked me to make the Sign of the Cross
over him. When I had done so I said, 'Kneel down
now, my sweet brother. . . . In a moment you will have
entered into life eternal. . . .' He murmured nothing
but the name of Jesus; and as he was speaking, I received his head into my hands."

But not all of Catherine's relationships were simple;
even among the Caterinati there were jealousies, and
some of the townspeople reviled the group, accusing
them of immorality. There is a legend, whether or not
it be true, that one such accuser lost his voice, and in
terror rushed to Catherine, who blessed him. He joined
the company he had reviled.

Though a number of her male disciples seem to have
acted as her secretaries, some became friends and messengers. Her relations with women differed considerably from those with the men in the group, whether
the latter were lay or clerical. Her feminine compan-

ions and devotees were numerous; but their personalities have not survived for our study as have those of the men, with three exceptions: one, a relative, Lisa; and the other two wealthy widows, Cecca Gori and Alessa Saracini. Alessa seems to have taught Catherine a great deal, among other things, how to read. She also gave her the opportunity of getting away from the noisy Benincasa home, and provided a quiet house where the fellowship could assemble in comfort. There is no doubt of the genuine spirituality of all who attached themselves to the company, nor of its consistently high idealism. Her disciples could not have sustained the heights she required of them had it not been so.

The Dominican friars at San Domenico, however, originally had little sympathy for her. They found her almost trance-like prayer embarrassing. Once a young brother who thought she was faking a rapture thrust a long needle into her foot; she neither moved nor groaned. But when she rose to walk, the wound gave her great pain.

A summons came from the Master General for Catherine to appear before the chapter in Florence to explain her living with so little food (rumor had it she lived exclusively on the host given her at Communion). Some believed she ate in secret, and that she was a hypocrite. But worst of all, she was a young woman who was teaching and leading others in the ways of the Holy Spirit. Her appearance before the chapter ended with her making new friends. No limitation was placed on anything she wished to do. The only requirement made by the order was that she accept for her confessor and guide Fra Raimondo della Vigne de Capua, a learned man of holy life who became her first biographer.

Even her own family became involved in her charities. In his joy over the confidence given his daughter, Giacomo Benincasa told her she could give what she wished to the poor. All his life she had been charitable, but he was not prepared for the lavish literalness with which she took him at his word. Barrels of flour and quantities of clothes disappeared. Her mother, Lapa, was scandalized one day to see her daughter in her white robe only; the black mantle was gone. For any woman to appear on the street without some sort of cloak marked her as an outcast from society. "I gave it to a half-naked beggar," said Catherine calmly. "Better to be without a cloak than without charity."

On one occasion two learned theologians came to question her and to set a trap. After answering their questions for a time she turned to them and said, "Learned fathers, in this science of doctrine you present but the shell of Christianity. Its kernel lies in the manner of one's life, in serving others." Both men were struck with embarrassment; for they lived in lordly luxury, even though one of them was a Franciscan provincial. He rose, took from his pouch a bunch of keys, and gave them to two young men who were following him. "For the love of God," he said, "go to my room and distribute all that is in it; and leave me nothing but my breviary."

One day word was sent to Father Raimondo, her director, that Catherine was dead. They had found her lying lifeless on her couch. A sick lay brother flung himself on the tiles beside the couch, and as he did so a gush of blood spouted from his lungs. Alessa, fearful for his life, tried to draw him away. But the man seized Catherine's hand and pressed it to his lips. Immediately the hemorrhage ceased, and at the same instant Catherine's eyelids lifted and she returned to consciousness. Turning her face to the wall she broke into bitter sobs and could not be comforted. All she would say was, "I saw the hidden things of God, and now I am thrust back into the prison of the body."

While Catherine and her little group of followers were engaged in prayer and the corporal works of mercy, the war between the free cities increased. In Siena the government of the twelve fell, and every one who had been a party to it was in danger. A neighbor rushed to the Benincasa house. Grasping Bartolomeo and his brother by the arm he shouted, "You must fly at once to the church of San Antonio; all are taking refuge there."

Catherine said, "No, not there. All who hide in San Antonio are lost. Come with me, and fear not." Half covering her brothers with her mantle she led them up the steep street to the Hospital of Mercy, placing them under the protection of the rector. Things developed as she had said; all the refugees at San Antonio were set upon and slain.

Catholic historians today are not particularly enthusiastic about the Crusades; but Catherine lived in a different age, one in which the divisions in Christendom were serious. When Gregory XI began to prepare the way for a crusade in 1372, Catherine rejoiced. She considered it a challenge for the church to shake off her

sloth, and to undergo hardship for the right. A united
Italy, with warring city states joining in a single endeavor, a united Christendom with peace won through
a holy war: these were the majestic (if erroneous) con-
ceptions which filled her mind. Because she felt that
national hatred would go down before an international
crusade, she flung herself into its support. It was,
perhaps, a simplistic belief that princes, condottieri,
and ordinary men-at-arms who seemed to love fighting
would do better to march against the infidel than to
wage civil war against their Christian brothers, as she
saw them doing. The crusade became for Catherine a
matter which was to occupy her for the rest of her life,
and the fact that it did not materialize was one of her
great disappointments.

In 1375 she was invited to Pisa to consult with its
leader, Bernabo Visconti, a cruel man, but an intelligent politician who was interested in obtaining an
alliance with the Tuscan republics of Pisa, Lucca,
Siena, Florence, and Arezzo. These republics were
adherents of the papal party, although it would have
needed little to tip the allegiance in the opposite direction.

Visconti tried to justify his claims over the church in
his domain. Catherine answered him, "Stupid is he
who revolts against that Vicar who holds the keys of
Christ crucified. . . . If the Vicar fails in his duty (he
ought to carry it out; it is an evil thing if he fails), we
must humbly await punishment and correction from
the sovereign judge, God eternal."

There is no question that Catherine was aware of the

deep-seated ecclesiastical corruption at this particular time. She wrote in the *Dialogue*, "Marvel at the private possessions and sums of money which each one keeps in private. These men wish only to fatten themselves and their cattle, while their poor brother dies of cold and hunger."

At the same time she felt strongly that rebellion against the church, however corrupt the church might be, could never be justified. She said clearly that the rebellious policy of Florence was inexcusable; but on the other hand, the behavior of the pope and the churchmen was also "devilish." Therefore, she saw the only means of peace to be such changes on the part of the church as to rid the rebels of any apparent excuse for their actions.

She was unsuccessful in her attempts through letters to the pontiff in Avignon to make peace with the citizens of Florence. Hardly had 1376 begun when word came that the pope had further irritated his Italian subjects by the type of churchmen he had chosen as nine new cardinals. Not only were seven of them French, but among them was the unscrupulous and hated Gerard du Puy, the Abbot of Mamoutier in Perugia. In a passion of protest Catherine dictated a letter to the pope repudiating his choice. The letter became famous; and quite rightly so when one recalls that Catherine, an uneducated young woman, was addressing the highest single authority in the Western world. She wrote, "I have heard that you have created cardinals. I believe it would be more to the honor of God and better for yourself if you would always take care to choose virtuous men. When the contrary is done it is a great insult to God and disaster to Holy Church."

The pope replied by excommunicating Florence for refusing to submit to the papal legates' rule (and tax) It was a disastrous move for the Florentines, since partly because of a genuine spirit of religious obedience, and partly because the condemned city state was threatened with the loss of its markets, an interdict worked far more efficiently than modern economic sanctions. For a state like Florence it spelled ruin. In desperation the Florentines asked Catherine to be mediator between themselves and the head of the church; for her reputation for sanctity would precede her, and she was already corresponding with the pope. Unfortunately, although she did not realize it when she accepted the mission, her appointment was unofficial; and the rulers of the city had not formally agreed to her as the city's representative.

1376 was, however, the momentous year of Catherine's life. She set out for Avignon with Neri, three Mantellate, Fra Bartolomeo, and Stefano Maconi. By the end of May the group was enlarged to 23.

When the entourage arrived in Avignon she discovered that an audience was not so easily granted; but she wrote a letter which came close to spiritual blackmail when it warned, "See to it that I do not have to appeal to Christ against you." She was forthright in stating what she believed to be the divine will: the pope was to make peace with the whole of Tuscany, and, in general, to clean up his own house. But what was most important to Catherine was that the pope should leave Avignon.

Eventually she was granted an audience, although it was made clear to her that since she had no official papers she could not be regarded as a representative for the Florentines. Catherine made short work of that problem: she spoke for Christ, and that was sufficient for her.

Her celebrated interview is recorded, and it is obvious that Catherine's reverence for the pontiff's person was sincere throughout. She spoke of the problems of Florence and of the desire of the people for reconciliation. When she had finished Pope Gregory remarked, "What you have done and said is good; I entrust the matter to you." There was an astonished protest from the cardinals present, but Catherine ignored them as she hurried to tell the pope the real purpose of her presence. She strongly urged a reform within ecclesiastical circles, describing in exact detail the corruption she had found in Avignon. The pope asked with an ironic smile how long she had been in the city; and she replied relentlessly, "Two days, your Holiness, but I make bold to say that I have perceived more wickedness and luxury here in that time than in my entire life in Siena."

She left the audience not knowing whether she had made any impression or not, but the next day she was visited by a number of cardinals who said they were sent from the pope to find out if the Florentines had really sent her. It seemed strange to them that Florence had no man capable of such an important mission.

Catherine answered calmly, and led them to their real point, which was the challenge she had thrown down. The delegation left, and the next day a papal messenger came to bring her to Gregory in his private apartments. He told her he regretted the persecution she had endured the day before, and assured her that the cardinals had questioned her against his wish. He granted her unusual spiritual and temporal favors in Avignon: a portable altar, three confessors for her disciples, lodging for her and her company, and money for her journey back to Italy.

But this was not what Catherine wanted. She urged him again to return to Rome and to reform the church. When he gave her reasons why leaving Avignon was impractical, she said with incredible authority, "You know what you promised God; now keep your vow."

The official account of the interview records that the pope turned pale, covered his face, and gasped, "It is true, it is true. To bring the Curia to Rome—that promise I made and have not kept, and must." Then he stared at Catherine. "How could you know that? I spoke to no one but God." She did not answer him, but before she left Gregory that day he had given her his word: he would return to Rome.

Catherine realized that Gregory was a good man, but a weak, vacillating, and tortured one. Every day she sent a messenger to him, and finally a letter was effective. In it she said, "I implore you on the part of Christ Crucified to make haste. Use a holy deceit; that is, appear to defer the day, but go quickly and soon, and you will escape this anguish and travail. Go quickly without any fear; if God is with you, no one is against you."

On September 13 the pope and Catherine and her group left Avignon. Deathly pale but resolute, Gregory XI stepped forth from the fortress castle. The Babylonian Captivity was over; the pope had left Avignon. For 70 years the greatest minds and hearts in Christendom had striven for this—Dante, Petrarch, Bridget of Sweden, Rienzi, statesmen, prelates—but it was Catherine of Siena who brought the pope back to Rome.

Both parties were delayed by scenes of violence, which did not worry Catherine but upset Gregory terribly. When the papal party arrived in Genoa, Catherine's entourage arrived at the same time. The biographer Caffarini is the only one who reports that, disguised as a simple priest, Gregory went to consult with Catherine. The news of war and insurrection throughout Italy frightened him; and he was tempted to return to peaceful, comfortable Avignon. What Catherine said to him in that secret meeting remains unknown; we only know that Gregory continued on the road to Rome. Perhaps she repeated what she had told him in a letter: "God looks to you to do his will; be a man."

The attitude toward Florence was reversed; peace was signed at the end of July, and Catherine left Florence for Siena—but not before she had told the Florentine government what she thought of their selfishness and betrayal of her.

Gregory's years in Rome were difficult. He hated the Italian climate, the Italian food, and Italian customs.

His delicate health deteriorated rapidly, and in a few years it was obvious he was dying. Whether or not he foresaw the disasters which were to come to the church after his death, he did make special arrangements for a quick election of a successor in Italy. He also guaranteed that the papal treasury and the keys of Castel Sant' Angelo would be safeguarded. On March 27, 1378 Gregory XI, who had reigned for less than eight years, died at the early age of 48.

The plans for a peaceful election came to nothing; for when the cardinals assembled a mob of Romans pressed around them, demanding the election of a Roman and making dire threats if their will was not honored. The cardinals thought first of postponing the election, and giving the crowd a mock pope; but the Cardinal of Aragon influenced them not to give way to fear, and they settled on a prelate of high reputation, one who was not even a cardinal: the Archbishop of Bari, Bartolomeo Prignano. To what extent they did so freely, and to what extent they felt forced to take him as a compromise candidate no one will ever know. In any case, he was canonically elected.

But the crowd misunderstood the announcement, hearing instead of the Archbishop of Bari, Archbishop de Bar, a Frenchman whom they hated; and a riot seemed imminent. Nothing came of it, however; the storm died down, and the Archbishop of Bari was enthroned as Urban VI. All should have gone well, and Catherine should have been able to return to her life of prayer and good works.

Unfortunately it was not so simple. Urban was without question an excellent man with the deepest horror of the simony, nepotism, laxity and vice which prevailed amongst the highest and lowest. But he had an ungovernable temper; he insulted and screamed at cardinals, bishops and any cleric who disagreed with his plans for reform. He called one cardinal a blockhead, another a liar, and in one consistory shouted at the gathered princes of the church to "Shut up." The cardinals left Rome; and on August 9, thirteen of them issued a letter declaring Urban VI a usurper, since he had only been elected because of their fear of the populace. Then they moved on to Fundi, where on September 20 they met in conclave to elect Cardinal Robert of Geneva as Clement VII, thus beginning the great schism which split the church into Urbanists and Clementines, a schism which was to plague the church for 70 years.

Anyone less dedicated than Catherine might well have given up, wondering whether the new development was not as bad as the papal residence in Avignon, and whether she might not have done better to have left well enough alone. But that was not Catherine's way. She returned to Rome, and with vigor, eloquence and logic threw the whole weight of her personality into the fight for Urban. She urged him to control his temper, to be lenient with those who opposed him, and to continue to pray and work for the reform of the church, but to do so as a shepherd and father. Urban respected her; and while she was able to restrain him to a degree, his native temperament was such that at times, especially after her death, his lack of control developed into an almost psychopathic desire for revenge.

Mary Hester Valentine

In her last year in Rome Catherine continued to dictate her *Dialogue,* and it is surprising how many spiritual phrases familiar to contemporary Catholics come from that book: "All the way to heaven is heaven, for he said I am the Way." "Time is the point of the needle." One wonders whether those who wrote the recent popular song realized the first line comes from Catherine's statement of her purpose in Rome, to be "like a bridge over troubled waters. . . ."

Although Catherine was only 33 in 1380, time was running out for her. The years of penance, travel, prayer and fasting had taken their toll. Her mother, Lapa, who had once resented the character of her daughter's life, now joined her, and even became a Dominican Tertiary. She joined Catherine in Rome; and was with her there for as long as she lived in the Eternal City, which was not very long. Catherine became ill in January, offering her fever and pain for peace in the church and the world. On April 29, 1380, bowing her head like her divine Master, she said quietly, "Father, into your hands I commit my spirit;" and as she said it, she died. The stigmata which she had received in Pisa during an ecstasy, and which she had prayed be invisible, showed clearly for all to see. She lies buried under the high altar in Santa Maria sopra Minerva.

This account of Catherine is obviously superficial, since it does not cover the mystical experiences she had in prayer and the miracles she performed, sometimes almost in spite of herself, as she concentrated on her work for the church and the papacy in a time when such dedication was sorely needed—as, indeed, it is in our own day. We can not imitate her ecstasies, since they were extraordinary spiritual gifts of God, but we can follow in her active life her love of the poor and devotion to the church. The important thing to remember is that her freedom to say exactly what she thought to popes, cardinals, bishops and clergy was counter-balanced by her patent orthodoxy. As de la Bedoyere points out, it was her vivid sense of the difference between what the church was and how too many of her human ministers behaved which was behind her freedom of speech, and which led her to rush into a very masculine world, paying no attention to distinction of sex, class or rank.

Pius II canonized her in 1468, and in 1939 Pius XII designated her the patron saint of Italy.

St. Joan of Arc
1412–1431

EVERYONE knows about Joan of Arc. She is a legend, a fairy tale, a mysterious little girl who died for her convictions. Her trial has been fully documented, as has her re-trial, but she remains a mystery. There is no one quite like her in Western history. The early girl martyrs—Agnes, Cecilia, even Joan's "saints," Catherine and Margaret—remain to us as vague memories of an ancient Roman period of persecution with the Coliseum as background and Nero or Diocletion as villains. We know them for what they represent of early Roman Christianity. Joan, however, lived in a specific geographic area; and her home may be visited today. She won real battles, and crowned a French king. But with her even the facts challenge the imagination, so that one person's Joan is quite different from another's.

There are, then, two Joans: the one of legend and the one of reality. St. Beuve insists that the former is full of sentimentality; but everything suggests that the other Joan was of a very different type, a realistic, often drastic, strong-willed, purposeful young woman.

But what was she really like? Did she really see visions? What impelled the dauphin of France to make her, a woman and only 17 years old, his commanding general? What made some of France's proudest soldiers follow her to the siege of Orleans? Did she have a fair trial? Why was the French church so afraid of her? And was she, as George Bernard Shaw insists, the first Protestant martyr?

So teasing, and so important for us today, are the historical, psychological and theological questions her life raises that a whole library of books about her has accumulated in the 500 years since her death, including historical commentaries, biographies, essays, plays, poems, historical novels.

John Cardinal Wright, who gave the panegyric in Orleans on the 537th anniversary of her liberating the city, had over 3,000 volumes on St. Joan in his personal library. Shakespeare, Voltaire, Schiller, Lang, Mark Twain, Anatole France, Shaw, Anouilh, and numerous others less famous have demonstrated by their writing about her that minds throughout the centuries find her as dynamic and challenging as did the people of her own time. There is a greatness and majesty in her life, and every attempt to present her as a young woman whose highest quality was sound common sense is pitiful.

The germ of Joan's story was planted long before she was born, when the English king, Edward III captured Calais, assumed the title "King of France," and continued to attack the country. Almost immediately after this take-over, an even more serious disaster overtook the land: the Black Death, which weakened French resistance even more. In the decisive victory at Poitiers after the Black Death, the Black Prince captured the French king, John II; and the French in 1360 were compelled to pay an enormous ransom for his release and to cede a number of important provinces to the English. At the same time John II conferred the fief of Burgundy on his younger son, Philip, which caused an inner division that took centuries to bridge.

All of Normandy was under English rule as an English province. The abbots of the Norman monastery were convinced that France would never rise except under English leadership, a "Vichy" policy which actually culminated in the trial, later, of Joan of Arc in Rouen.

But the military and heroic side of the Hundred Years War, according to Sven Stolpe, has been over-emphasized in both English and French documents. Actually, from the very beginning, the war was part of the eternal struggle for the southern Low Countries, where English wool was converted into precious and useful Flemish cloth.

As is the case in Central America and the Middle East today, the war was especially cruel to the poor farmers. Year after year they were plundered by the combatants and innumerable bands of brigands. Lawlessness reigned; agriculture was paralyzed; and many, even of the formerly well-to-do, starved. This is the *"grande pitie"* of which Joan of Arc spoke at her trial.

As in Germany after the Versailles treaty, the monetary unit sank to one twelve-thousandth of its former value. A chicken which in normal times would cost four francs now cost 40,000 francs, and one is reminded of the German farmer in 1929 who complained that his cow would only buy a herring.

It was into this world of conflict that the girl whom they called Joan was born on Epiphany, 1412, to Jacques d'Arc and his wife Isabel of Domremy, Lorraine. She had two elder brothers, Jacques and Jean; and a sister,

Catherine. The house in which Joan was born still remains, although it has been altered and enlarged. What is important is that it still stands, close to the church of St. Remy where Joan often prayed.

The little girl grew up tall and sturdy, of strong body and clear mind. She never went to school. She could neither read nor write; but her mother taught her the Lord's Prayer, the Ave Maria, and the Creed; and she loved hearing about the lives of the saints. During the trial of Joan numerous incidents from her childhood came out, giving a fairly clear picture of those early days. She has been called a shepherdess, but she herself said she preferred household duties to tending the flocks. She proudly told her judges that there was no woman in Rouen whom she could not equal in needlecraft.

We also know that she took care of the poor; that she had to be prevented from sleeping on the floor and giving up her own bed to the sick; that she nursed the sick; and that, in the words of her playmates, "She was so wonderfully kind."

In the meantime the political upheaval continued in the country, and Domremy sided not with the Burgundians but with the French. Obviously all the details of the struggle were discussed in the marketplace and the kitchens of Domremy. Her childhood must have been filled with tales of violence and murder, attacks and plunderings; and her youth was filled with tension and anxiety.

One morning when she was thirteen she went into the meadow to gather flowers with her playmates, and a dazzling light shone by her, and she heard voices. The first message, she testified later, told her that she must be a good girl and pray frequently. Then the voices spoke to her more often of faith and its observance; and eventually they gave her a clear order which was to change not only her life but those of countless others, including the dauphin and the ecclesiastics of Rouen, and the fate of two countries.

By now she could identify the voices as those of St. Catherine, St. Margaret, and the Archangel Michael; but which one gave her the decisive order she never revealed. At any rate, it was a frightening commission: "Daughter of God, you must lead the dauphin to Rheims, so that he may be crowned in the right manner." Anatole France says, "The girl listened. The mists cleared, and the shining light spread in her soul. . . . It was for this that she had been chosen by God."

But it was not as simple as that. She resisted the call for three years, for she was clear-sighted enough to realize the near impossibility of the order. Her parents would certainly not agree to her leaving on such a senseless mission. Certainly she was no camp follower and she had practical doubts about the soldiers' accepting her on such slim evidence as voices. Her spiritual development, like that of all the saints, was a slowly awakening awareness that what she accomplished would be done, not through her, but through the guidance of God. Hers was a hard moral schooling, through obedience to her voices and her inner conscience, as well as through the asceticism which was obvious even to her family. Keeping her inner life secret, she advanced to the point where she could accept the directive with the martyrdom it implied. But this was four years after she first heard the voices. It was 1428, and she was not yet 17 years old.

On All Saints night of the same year, the unfortunate Charles VII, a timid, melancholy fellow, filled with self doubt, knelt in his chapel and asked a despairing question of God. Should he continue as king or not? He was the son of mad Charles VI; but his Bavarian mother, Isabeau, refused to acknowledge or disavow his legitimacy. On the other hand, the English king, Henry VI, was the unquestioned son of the French Princess Catherine and Henry V, and had been legitimately elected. Many have argued whether or not Charles himself had a vision (he never said), but the fact is that he clung to the throne against all the odds.

And, back in Domremy, Joan finally accepted her heavenly orders. Her voices told her to go to the captain, Robert de Baudricourt, in the town of Vaucouleurs. He would provide her with soldiers who would take her to the dauphin. She slipped away from home, reached Baudricourt, and convinced that hard-bitten soldier of the truth of her message. Certainly it was worth a try; things could not possibly be any worse.

On February 12, 1429, with Jean de Metz as guide, she was ready to depart. She had cut her hair short and wore male clothing and armour, and de Baudricourt himself presented her with a sword and a charger and made her escort swear on earth to protect her. She had pointed out, realistically, that it was best for both her and her companions were she not dressed as a woman. The records show that she compelled the unquestioning respect of her companions. Dunois, who was very close to her, testified that he did not think any woman could be more chaste than the Maid. Clearly, for her, garb had a symbolic meaning: she had sworn chastity, but her mission was of a warlike nature.

Near Chinon, where the king resided, she heard three masses at the church of St. Catherine, and spent most of the morning there in prayer. That evening the king granted permission for her party to enter Chinon.

There is a legend that Joan of Arc identified Charles miraculously. This would have been unnecessary, for everybody in the country recognized the king; and Joan would have learned all there was to know. We have a record of what she did say: "Most illustrious Sir Dauphin, I have been sent from God to bring help to the kingdom and to yourself." It was as simple as that.

Charles, naturally, was cautious; there were women accused of witchcraft in the country, and he did not want his reputation further blemished by contact with one of these. He had her questioned by theologians at Poitiers concerning her mission and her claim. It was a long examination, and a wearying one. She told them four things which would result from her mission: she would relieve Orleans; the dauphin would be crowned in Rheims; Paris would return to the king; and the Duke of Orleans, captive in the Tower of London, would return home. The examiners' report to the king was that they could find no evil in her, only "goodness, humility, virginity, devotedness, honesty, and simplicity."

The king conferred the command of the army upon Joan. In Rouen he placed ten to twelve thousand men at her disposal, and gave her his own staff and the standard of a commander-in-chief: it depicted the King of Heaven holding the world in one hand, with the other raised in

Mary Hester Valentine

benediction. Kneeling were St. Michael and Gabriel with *fleurs de lis*, and the motto was "Jesus! Marie!" So Joan went forth with the assurance that "In God's name soldiers will fight, and God will give the victory."

It was war; and while we know the outcome, Joan experienced the reality with all its horrors. She led the army, but said, "I have never killed anybody." She took care never to allow herself to hate the English or the Burgundians, but she knew where her loyalties lay. In nine months she would accomplish a task which has no parallel in the world's history. She would coordinate an army which until then had retreated more often than it had advanced. She allowed no swearing, loathed women who followed the soldiers, and was easily angered at evil. A story is told that when she heard a knight swearing and blaspheming she became so indignant that she seized him by the collar and cried out that she would not let him go unless he promised never to use such language again. The alarmed knight promptly assured her that he would never again be guilty of bad language. The night before the decisive battle she ordered the population of the town and garrison to confess and receive Communion; and even the tough warrior, La Hire, did so.

To the king, who questioned her about her voices, she said, "When I feel sad because I am not easily believed I go away and lay the matter before the Lord, and express my grief that those to whom I talk do not believe me. And when I have ended my prayer I hear a voice which says, 'Daughter of God, go,' and then I feel great happiness."

We know the outcome, but for Joan and the troops it was no battle of Jericho. No walls came tumbling down at the blowing of trumpets. Like all war the battle was brutal and bloody, and many on both sides died in agony. Joan herself was wounded, and cried spontaneously and unashamed as she drew out the arrow which had pierced her. When the bridge on which the English commander, Glasdale, and his troops were retreating collapsed, she knelt down to pray for her unhappy enemies, while tears ran down her cheeks. She found priests for the dying, and cradled a wounded Englishman in her arms until he died. Her own troops were encouraged by the sight of her banner; and, shouting "For France and the Maid," they succeeded where those who had preceded them had failed. Orleans was freed; and then it was on to Rheims where the king was crowned, for those were the clear orders she had received from her voices. Nothing else was her aim. At the coronation she knelt before him in the presence of all the great lords, and said, "Now the will of God is done."

After this the voices never gave any more orders for the field; everything she did after that was at the counseling of human voices. As a matter of fact, her successes ended with the coronation at Rheims.

But this is not surprising, for the saving of France demanded a supernatural intervention. In Easter week, 1430, Sts. Catherine and Margaret appeared before her, speaking a new message. "Before midsummer day you will be taken captive, for so it is decreed. But do not fear; take all well, for God will be your aid."

And so it was. She was captured at Compiegne; and although her long agony begins at this point, it is from now on that she begins to rise to the real heights of sanctity. We cannot understand the supreme logic of Joan's life if we do not recognize it as an imitation of Christ. From her childhood she had moved always closer to God; now she would experience his suffering and death in order to become united with him.

She was a valuable prisoner: the English had paid 10,000 livres for her; ten or twelve francs was the price of a horse.

The record of the trial of Joan is one of the most celebrated documents of history. Reading it is a shocking experience, since it makes us witnesses of a drama of the deepest pathos where innocence and youth were victims of political passion and theological and juridical chicanery. Formal law triumphed over candor and intuition.

Nearly all the judges were at one time or other on the English payroll, through ecclesiastical appointments that were in the hands of the English king. Joan was thus pitted against 60 skilled politicians, lawyers, and ambassadors, trained in all the complexities of legal questioning. All were versed in academic casuistry; and most of them were avowedly her enemies—especially Cauchon, to whom Joan said, "Take care what you do, for I am in truth sent by God, and you are placing yourself in great peril."

Yet, ill-prepared though she was to dialogue with these subtle masters of language, her answers as recorded have fascinated readers for the past 500 years. When asked if she thought she was in the state of grace she answered, "If I am not, I pray God to make me so; and if I am, may God keep me so." Then she adds a thought which shows that she had pondered her problems: "If I were in a state of sin I do not believe the Voices would come to me. . . . I wish that everyone understood that as well as I do."

Asked what the voices told her about the salvation of her soul she said, "They told me to be good, to go to church often." To the Dominican, Seguin, who asked Joan what language her voices spoke, Joan replied, "A better French than yours, Sire." (Seguin spoke in Limousin dialect.) Asked if she would submit her life, acts and sayings, either good or evil, to the decision of the church, she replied, "I commit myself to Our Lord, who sent me, to Our Lady, and to all the blessed saints of paradise." She added that since Our Lord and the church were all one her judges were making difficulties where there were none, and then pleaded, "Let all I have said and done be sent to Rome to our Holy Father, the pope, to whom after God I refer myself. I refer me to God and to our Holy Father." It was Holy Week.

What is obvious to anyone who reads the entire trial (it took five months) is that, throughout, Joan attempted to translate her spiritual experiences in faltering human language. She found it difficult to formulate theories and opinions. To her, religion was simplified to a few things: clarity of vision in her revelations, absolute obedience to the voices which spoke the will of God, love of the Savior who had sacrificed himself for her, and love of the suffering people around her. It was as simple as that. As one of her biographers notes, "Joan is one of the few examples of a soul that possesses holiness without being aware of it.

The only thing she knew was the will of God and the aims which he wished to realize through her."

At the end of the trial she was told, "Sign this document and you will be released." We do not know how much she had understood, or whether the meaning of the recantation was clear to her. An English cleric, Laurent Calot, came up to the stand, crumbled the original document, drew another out of his sleeve, and laid it before Joan. "But I can neither read nor write," she said.

Calot, nevertheless, handed her a pen with which she smilingly drew a ring on the paper. Calot then took her hand and guided it to form a cross and signature at the foot of the recantation, which expressly stated that Joan rejected her revelations and voices. Nowhere is the cold-blooded judicial murder more evident than here. Between Joan and her judges was an abyss: her innocent candor.

She was accused of heresy, witchcraft, and of immodesty in wearing men's clothing. She had accepted women's clothing in prison, but resumed her armor as protection when the guards attempted to rape her.

There are references to an iron cage in which she could not hold herself straight, but this cannot be confirmed. What is certain is that she was chained by the neck, hands and feet. She was alone in the prison tower, surrounded by brutal soldiers who insulted and wounded her. When she was returned to prison at the trial's end the warder's brutality increased. She was beaten until blood flowed; and when the commission entered they found her almost unrecognizable, bloody, her face ravaged, her hair close-cropped.

St. Joan of Arc

When Martin Laurenu informed Joan that she was to be burnt alive, she burst into tears. "Oh, that I should be treated so cruelly. Oh, that my body which has never been defiled should today be consumed and become ashes. Before God, the highest judge, I appeal against these acts of violence." At that moment Cauchon entered; and she cried, "My Lord Bishop, it is you who murder me."

At eight in the morning she was released from her fetters and dressed in a long linen garment. On her head was placed a cap in the shape of a mitre, on which was written the declaration: "Heretic, relapsed, apostate, idolater." She mounted the cart.

She was led to the stake. Jean Massieur describes the event succinctly: "While I was doing my best to comfort her on the scaffold an English captain said to me, 'What, priest, are you going to keep us here until dinnertime?' Then without any formality, or any reading of the sentence, they dispatched her straight to the fire, saying to the executioner, 'Do your duty.' And so, while she was still uttering praise and lamentations to God and the saints, she was led off and tied to the stake. She had me hold up the Crucifix before her eyes, so that the cross on which God hung should be continually before her, so long as her life lasted. Her last word as she died was a loud cry of 'Jesus.'" She was 20 years old.

The executioner collected her ashes and threw them into the Seine, lest people might believe she had escaped.

Jean Alepee, canon of Rouen, wept, saying, "I wish my soul were where the soul of that woman is;" and one of the English, John Tressart, said loudly, "We are lost; we have burned a saint."

And where was Charles, upon whom the Maid had placed a crown, during these months of trial and final execution? When she was captured by the Burgundians and turned over to the English, Charles did not lift a finger to save her from being burned as a heretic.

Her mother, however, remembered her lovely little daughter, her prayerful child whose only desire was "to be good." She grieved for twenty years, but never forgot her, nor gave up her firm determination to have her good name restored. Joan was not to be remembered by history as an evil woman, a heretic and a witch if her mother could do anything about it. She continued to plead with those who had access to the king, and her prayers to God were for the restoration of the good name of her daughter who had served him so completely, even to death.

Finally, early in 1450, two years before the defeat of the English and the end of the Hundred Years' War, and nearly 20 years after Joan's death, King Charles VII, having captured Rouen, requested Guillaume Bouille, rector of the University of Paris, to begin an investigation of the trial of Joan, the Maid. He wished to know the truth of the matter, and to learn the manner in which the proceedings had been conducted. After the testimony of Guillaume Manchon, the principal scribe who had taken the original proceedings, and that of six other witnesses, a report was made to the king indicating that the trial had been invalid.

Two years later the church began an official investigation. As a result, Pope Callixtus III gave permission in June, 1455, for Joan's mother and her brothers, Pierre and Jean, to enter a suit for her rehabilitation. Brehal, in 1456, drew up an impressive document of indictment of the original trial. In July, 1456, in the name of the pope, the Archbishop of Rheims, at a solemn ceremony, declared formally that the original trial and sentence were "contaminated with fraud, calumny, wickedness, contradictions, and manifest errors of fact and law," and restored Joan's good name in the church.

Manchon, a witness and senior clerk to the original trial, declared at the rehabilitation that those who dared oppose Cauchon fled for their lives. His testimony is without doubt the most important material we possess concerning the trial. He states categorically, "Those in charge of the conduct of the case, that is to say, my Lord of Beauvais and the lawyers whom they summoned from Paris for the purpose, and also the English at whose instance the case was started, acted out of hatred and contempt for the King of France." He notes, "At the beginning . . . when I was writing down the Maid's answer and excuses, the judges tried to compel me to alter my words in translating them into Latin, thereby changing the meaning of her statements into something quite different from my understanding of them."

Pierre Miget testified that d'Estivet very often abused Joan, calling her a loose woman and a filthy creature, while Jean Massieu insisted that the abjuration was not the one quoted in the report of the case.

Her squire declared, "All the Maid's exploits seemed to me rather divine and miraculous than otherwise. It would have been impossible for any one as young as the Maid to perform such deeds except at the will and guidance of Our Lord."

Marguerite La Rouroulde, with whom Joan lived after the coronation, described her impressions in detail. For instance, once she said that perhaps the reason Joan never felt fear in battle was that she could not be killed. Joan immediately denied the suggestion. "I am no more immune to danger than any other soldier." In another incident, burghers' wives came to Marguerite's house and wished Joan to touch and bless their rosaries. Joan smiled and said to her hostess, "Touch them yourself, do! It will be just as effective."

Joan's godmother, Beatrice Estelin, noted that Joan was chaste and well-mannered, pious in her attendance at church. "In my opinion," she declared, "there was not a better girl in the two villages."

In short, the trial which condemned her was a farce brought by collaborators of the enemy and men of boundless ambition. It is filled with errors of fact.

Few have had such a sharp light focused upon their whole lives as Joan, few have been examined by such pitiless judges, and yet nothing in her life shows a trace of impurity or arrogance. She is an instrument; she obeys; she listens.

As Cardinal Wright pointed out, Joan is one of the very few not required to take the long road toward perfection. Her inner struggle took place mainly between thirteen and seventeen, after which she was purified. It was then that God cut short her triumph and reserved for her the greatest of all tasks, to be united with Christ in his own suffering, to become a martyr.

In 1920 Joan of Arc was canonized, not on the basis of her visions, because contact with supernatural spheres is a miracle and cannot be analyzed, but because she recognized God's call as her reason for being, a vocation so individual no one else could accomplish it. Today that same inspiration is given the individual conscience by the same God: we are all invited to follow Joan's unquestioning obedience.

And yet, brilliant and astounding as the truth about Joan of Arc is, she remains a mysterious figure of simple integrity. One of the amusing ironies of her story is that during World War I it was the English-speaking soldiers, crossing the Channel, who sang the then popular song, "Joan of Arc, we are calling you!"

And that brings me to a question I shall ask her when I see her, as I hope to some day, a question that has bothered me ever since as a child I heard the story of Joan of Arc: Why was God pro-French?

St. Teresa of Avila
1515–1582

O NE of the strange anomalies biographers of Teresa of Avila seem to fall into without even being aware of it, is their tendency to classify her as a mystic, an ecstatic given to swooning at prayer, having trances, even levitating. They delight in stories of her awe-struck nuns holding her down by the hem of her habit, as, saucepan in hand, she is overcome by a vision while she is preparing the evening meal. What is interesting about all this is that what they say is, for the most part, true; but it was the aspect of her life that Teresa herself most distrusted and was embarrassed by. With the exception, perhaps, of Allison Peers and Kate O'Brien, what few emphasize is what those who knew her best insisted upon: her intelligence, her great warmth, what fun it was to be with her, and how her presence made all around her merry.

It was she who remarked wryly about a serious candidate who had applied to join one of her convents, "I don't know; she is fairly melancholy, and a sad saint is a sad saint indeed." Dorothy Day in one of her columns noted that she had her radio on—Berlioz, Schubert, Chopin—as a pacifier, and then quoted St. Teresa as she grabbed her castanets and started to dance during the hour of recreation in her unheated convent, "One must do something to make life bearable!"

Even today her personality attracts those who read her own works rather than what others have said about her. Edith Stein became a Catholic after reading her life; and a famous Spanish scholar always ended his lecture on Teresa and her influence on the Spain of her day and every century since with the comment that Teresa "is so *human.*"

If this account errs, therefore, in stressing the humanity of Teresa, and merely touches on the extraordinary, it is only to get the picture of this extraordinary woman into a little better focus.

Teresa de Cepeda y Ahumada was born in the Castilian town of Avila in 1515, the year in which Martin Luther formulated his dogma of grace. Only recently, since the records of that period have been available to interested scholars, have we learned that Teresa's ancestors, although *hidalgos,* had bought that patent of nobility; and that her grandfather was a *converso,* that is, a Jew who had accepted baptism. Teresa's father was baptised when he was a little boy; and the family adopted a new name with their new status for safety's sake, and to guarantee their acceptance. Her father was proud of his position; and he was a pious, sincere Catholic, devoted to his family. Nothing of this Jewish background appears in Teresa's autobiography (written under obedience). Whether this was because she was unaware of it, or because it was more prudent during this period of the Inquisition to keep such dark family skeletons carefully stowed away in the closet of memory, we shall never know.

At any rate, her mother, Dona Beatriz Ahumada, Don Alonzo's second wife, was a true Spaniard and wealthy, owning farms and property around Avila. She had great beauty (which her daughter inherited) and loved to read novels, a "vice" she also passed on to Teresa. Cervantes in *Don Quixote* gives us not only the Spanish attitude toward romances during this period, but also the type of romances young Teresa was reading with her mother until the latter died when Teresa was 13. But it was not only the escapades of knights and fantastic novels of chivalry which the small Teresa read. She herself says, "We used to read the lives of the saints . . . and when I read of the martyrdoms suffered by saintly women for God's sake, I used to think that they had purchased . . . God very cheaply, and I had a keen desire to die as they had done."

There is the well-known story of how the child Teresa and her little brother, Rodrigo, discussed the possibility of becoming martyrs and agreed to go off to the country of the Moors, "begging our bread for the love of God so that they might behead us there." Peers points out that while hagiographers have told this story with relish as an indication of Teresa's early yearning which was expressed later in the saying "To suffer or to die, O Lord," it may well be simply a 16th century adaptation of our century's "Let's play Superman."

At any rate, she herself tells us that shortly after her mother's death she discarded reading the lives of the saints and began to dress so as to attract others,

"Taking great trouble with my hands and hair, using perfumes and all vanities of this kind I could get." But she adds, "I was never happy unless I had a new book;" and for those of us who are reading addicts this little note is refreshingly human.

She goes on to recall a relative, slightly older and considerably more sophisticated, who was a disturbing influence on Teresa—according to her father, so much so that he decided to send her to an uncle in the country, where she could benefit from the healthful atmosphere and her tendency to frivolity might be limited. Later he sent her to a boarding school for girls of good family, "Our Lady of Grace," where she spent eighteen months until the first of her serious and mysterious illnesses forced her worried father to bring her home. It all occurred too long ago and too far away to justify any modern conjectures on what the illness was. She herself called it "a great infirmity," and we would do well to leave it at that.

During her convalescence she reflected on her past life (one recalls Ignatius of Loyola's conversion while he was recovering from his battle wound); and, according to Teresa, "I began to fear that if I had died of my illness, I should have gone to hell . . . and I saw that being a nun was the best and safest state, so . . . I determined to force myself to embrace it." It was not an enthusiastic attraction to religious life; but, given Teresa's nature, it was a compelling one. She entered the Carmelite convent of the Incarnation in Avila on November 2, 1536, when she was 21; and she was professed a year later.

During the first year after taking vows Teresa became inexplicably ill. She does not appear to have been unhappy; but she became afflicted so seriously that her father obtained permission to take her to the mountains where, it was hoped, the clear air would cure her. Her illness increased, however; and the doctors diagnosed her a consumptive, a convenient medical cover-all then, as viruses are in our day. She was hurried back to Avila that she might die in the convent in which she was professed. Indeed, she was at one time pronounced dead and preparations were begun for her funeral. Fortunately, the calling together of the large family delayed the obsequies; and before she could be buried she opened her eyes and spoke. In one of those graphic touches in her autobiography she tells us that when she recovered consciousness she found wax on her eyelids! Her recovery was slow, however; and she remained an invalid for nearly three years more, participating when she could in the regular life of the convent.

This participation could not have been very onerous, for the convent of the Incarnation, like many in Spain at that time, was large, rich, and filled with younger daughters of aristocratic houses of Castile. It was not a den of iniquity; but lax it certainly was, in terms of the original Carmelite Rule, with parlors and gardens filled with visitors who had come to gossip, play games, and enjoy the good food which friends, relatives and benefactors provided.

For Teresa it was a period of tension: she found her allegiance divided between God and the world, and she was at peace with neither. "When I was in the midst of worldly pleasures I was distressed by the remembrance of what I owed to God; when I was with God I grew restless because of worldly affections." Then she adds a comment which "is so human." "Very often I was more occupied in wishing my hour of prayer were over, and in listening whenever the clock struck, than in thinking of things that were good." Even later, when prayer was the center of her life, she wrote of the thoughts like "little gnats which buzz around by night here and there."

"Against this evil I know no remedy," she said. "The sole remedy which I meet with, after having wearied myself for many is . . . to consider the memory no better than a mad man, and to leave it alone with its folly, for God alone can check its extravagances."

During the whole of 20 years she confined her spiritual exercises to meditation. Except after Communion she never attempted to pray without a book, and she admits that when she did so she experienced distractions and aridity. Prayer in the sense of communion with God, which "in my view is nothing but friendly intercourse with him who we know loves us," she gave up for a time altogether. Not until she was about 40 years old did the beginnings of sanctity manifest themselves. To use her own image, she "was a plant of slow growth, and needed a great deal of watering."

Then gradually her prayer life began to change, and with it a feeling of revulsion for the kind of women's club life that was the norm in the convent of the Incarnation. She found herself talking with God, and hearing him answer, "I will have you converse now not with men, but with angels." This statement greatly moved her, spoken as it was in the depths of the spirit.

St. Teresa of Avila

Without losing any of the engaging charm which had distinguished her from childhood she developed a determination, a decisiveness and fortitude, which few women in history have possessed. She saw clearly that the life she was to lead needed to be based upon the original Carmelite Rule of solitude, silence, fasting and abstinence from meat, with prescribed hours for contemplative prayer. She also realized that her companion sisters in the Incarnation had no such desire to leave their comfortable, relaxed way of life; and so with the help of relatives and friends she obtained a little house in north Avila and in 1562 founded the reformed convent of San Jose with five young novices.

But clouds were gathering. She began to have mystical experiences, and her confessors gave her conflicting advice. Continually in her writings she complains of the stupidity of priests who, whatever their sanctity, are not well enough educated to undertake spiritual direction, and whose norm was their own experience. Her comfort during this period was Christ himself, who assured her that he would not forsake her. Gradually she had other supporters: a Jesuit who assured her she was clearly being led by the Holy Spirit, and then the ascetic Franciscan, St. Peter of Alcantara, who was himself attempting to return to the primitive Franciscan Rule. Teresa found him "very affable, and when he did speak it was a delight to listen to him, for he was extremely intelligent." Besides giving Teresa moral support, Peter of Alcantara, who had contacts in high places, persuaded Pope Pius IV to authorize the founding of the new convent based upon the old Rule.

The city of Avila was furious, for if the newly formed house were to have no income it would be a burden on an already over-taxed municipality. This problem of income was to plague Teresa in each of her foundations, so much so that she frequently opened them at night under cover of darkness. It also explains her constant reference to an applicant's dowry in her letters and in the *Foundations*, although again delightful inconsistency constantly crops up. "If she is a good girl, even if she has no dowry and so sponsor, send her; God will provide." It is pleasant to record that after the initial problems the first five years of her great reform were comparatively happy ones.

Initially Teresa had to cope with the indignation of her companions at the Incarnation, who saw her withdrawal from their house as a personal insult, and the reluctance of the townspeople wherever she founded a new reformed convent, since they saw its lack of endowment as a threat to their own resources. She also had to face the Carmelite Father General, who was horrified that she had acted without formal permission. But she did have the approval of King Philip II, who welcomed a little more discipline and prayer in the religious houses in Spain. Eventually she won over her opponents; but it was an inch-by-inch, step-by-step affair, with the pattern of resistance repeated with varying emphases with each of the convents she founded.

A dramatic twist to her reforming zeal followed the official visit of the Carmelite Father General, who had come to close the experiments which were being talked about by friend and foe alike. His observation left him thoroughly won over, and so impressed that he talked with Teresa about the possibility of her founding similar reformed Carmelite monasteries for men. When one considers the position of women in Spain at that time it was an extraordinary request, but Teresa was equal to it. "Show me the men who are willing to give themselves unreservedly to you," she said to Christ; and the answer came almost immediately when Fray Antonio of Jesus, Joseph of Christ, and the future Saint John of the Cross indicated their desire to lead a more spiritually oriented life than was possible in their monasteries. They were given a house in Valladolid by a person of some importance (Teresa does not name the donor), with a fine large garden and a vineyard adjoining it. On November 28, 1568, the three men took their new vows, the first of a great company of discalced friars who even in the first decades of their history included many of unusual sanctity.

Teresa was kept busy for the next few years visiting her convents, traveling with one or other of her nuns in all weather on dusty or muddy roads in covered carts that bumped their way over the rugged terrain. They were forced frequently to stay overnight at the poor inns that dotted the countryside—a penance Teresa found more difficult than fasting, for she who loved neatness and cleanliness almost to excess found herself surrounded by filth and the noise of drunken, fighting muleteers.

In October, 1571, a surprising change came over her life; and for three years her reformed convents were on their own, as their foundress was assigned to return to her original convent of the Incarnation by the Apostolic Visitor. Things had been going from bad to worse at the Incarnation: the novitiate had been closed by the Father General, and the remaining nuns found themselves short of benefactors and equally short of food. Many of the "ladies" began to talk about returning to their homes, and the Apostolic Visitor decided that Teresa was the one person who might bring order and peace to the Incarnation were she its prioress.

It was an incredibly difficult position for Teresa; nine years before she had been the butt of ridicule by the very sisters she was now asked to lead. When she entered the choir, accompanied by the provincial, pandemonium broke out. The noise rose to shrieks as her supporters began to sing the *Te Deum* (rather loudly, one supposes), while the opposition attempted to shout them down. Teresa herself took no notice. She knelt in prayer before the altar, and then turned to face them; and when by the sheer force of her personality the tumult quieted down, she spoke to the 130 nuns whose prioress she was about to become. Her address was a model of tact and prudence, especially when one remembers that Teresa did not want this new position any more than her opponents among the sisters wanted her to have it.

"My ladies, Our Lord has sent me to this house in obedience to hold this office, which I never thought of, and which I am far from deserving. This election greatly distresses me, because it has laid upon me a task I am far from deserving. I shall be unable to perform it without your help; and it has deprived you of the freedom of election which you used to enjoy, and has given you a prioress whom you have not chosen. . . . I come to serve and please you in every way I can, and I hope the Lord will assist me in this. I am a daughter of this house, and a sister of you all. My desire is that we should all serve the Lord in quiet, and do the little which our Rule and Constitutions commend to us, for the love of that Lord to whom we owe so much."

There is a story lovingly honored by Carmel that the next day when the sisters came to Chapter they found a statue of Our Lady in the seat of the Prioress, and Teresa's own chair below it, on a level with that of the rest of the community. Pointing to the statue she is quoted as saying, "There is your Prioress; I am simply her servant."

It was an uphill fight, but Teresa by sheer force of personality and charm not only restored discipline to the Incarnation but also, through her business-like instincts, determination, and the friends who respected her, was able to return the house to its former prosperity. Part of her success, no doubt, also rested on the fact that healthy fun was a part of her nature; and she encouraged it in all her houses, not least of all in the Incarnation. She truly loved people, and admitted, "I have no defense against affection; I could be bribed with a sardine." She had no patience with the self-righteous. A visitor who found her happily eating a partridge some one had sent her was scandalized. Teresa actually enjoying her food; what would people think? "Let them think what they please," said Teresa.

"There is a time for partridge and a time for penance."
She disliked gloomy people and has left us a prayer to
be delivered from frowning saints.

Three years later a renewed Incarnation was able to
elect a successor to Teresa. Although the first ballot
went to Teresa she refused another term, presided at
the election of her substitute, and returned to her be-
loved convent of San Jose, Avila, with all its austerities.
The years as prioress at the Incarnation had been trying ones, but her growth in prayer was phenomenal
during this period. She seemed in almost constant communication with God; and one day when she was
praying about the needs of the house her Lord answered, "I have heard you; let me alone"—amusingly
similar to the line in the Psalm in which he says, "Be
still, know that I am God."

She began to have more frequent intellectual visions,
or, as we might perhaps say today, spiritual insights.
She says, "I was increasingly conscious of Christ, but
neither with the eyes of the body nor with those of the
soul did I see anything." God to her was not an idea,
but a present reality to be experienced in life. To her
the kingdom of God was truly within. We are all familiar with her statement that the Lord dwells among
the pots and pans, but we are perhaps less conscious of
her insistence that our reaching for God is a continuous
series of conversions, discoveries, infidelities and re-
pentance. Her teaching is parallel to that of contemporary theologians who teach us that the experience of
God is a decisive fact running the whole gamut of
human experiences, qualifying and Christianizing

them. For her, Martha and Mary always acted together.

To her sisters of the reform she stressed prayer as a matter of life or death. Nothing can substitute for it; and to one who admitted she had given up prayer Teresa remarked, "I know no remedy other than to begin praying again." To one who was impressed by her observation of Teresa's own prayer, and who asked what she could do to achieve such absorption in God, Teresa answered, "Say the Our Father, but take an hour to do it." It sounds very contemporary, and at the same time very scriptural, since it echoes Christ's warning about those who repeat many prayers while their hearts are far from God. As Segundo Galilea observes, her message is an alarm signal to those of us who have lost interest in advancing in prayer, or have consigned it to the shadowy edge of our Christian commitments. For Teresa it is a living thing, and like all living things is meant to grow.

As she advanced in age and wisdom she constantly warned that without a holy life and conformity to God's will here and now, prayer is practically impossible. Doing God's will was for her—as for all God's saints and, indeed, as it was for God's Son—the primary task.

In her writings, which she began under obedience at about this time, she speaks with amazing frankness and simplicity of her "interviews with God." At times he spoke with a bluntness very like her own, as when she complained to him of one of her characteristic faults, and he answered, "Daughter, there is no help for that!"

87

Mary Hester Valentine

Teresa's writings fall into two classes: those she wrote for the nuns of the reformed Carmel, plus 1500 letters to relatives, to whom she was always devoted, and to friends; and her life story, with all her spiritual experiences included, which she wrote unwillingly at the orders of her spiritual advisors. Allison Peers feels that the *Foundations*, the report of the establishment of the discalced convents, is the least interesting and certainly not the book one should read first to become acquainted with Teresa. I disagree with the eminent scholar. I began with the *Foundations* and was captivated by the amusing trivia with which they are filled: the advice to a sick sister to eat rhubarb regularly in the morning for her digestive difficulties, the recommendation to an impoverished house to weave straw coverlets for their beds since they are both waterproof (leaking roof?) and easily replaced. There is the wry advice to one of her prioresses not to let a lazy cook spoil the broth: "We eat little enough by rule; it ought at least be edible."

Teresa fancied herself a poet; but in this area, at least, her judgment failed her. At best she is a versifier, but occasional verse—and it was at this she excelled—is seldom more than that. One amusing example we have tells about her sense of humor and trust in God to work small miracles for his friends more than about her poetic abilities. The convent found to their horror that it was infested with "little beasties." A benefactor had just supplied the nuns with new frieze habits, and they feared their new clothes might become infested. Teresa organized a procession with a long verse prayer which listed the problems the creatures presented in graphic detail, each stanza ending with:

> Since thou givest us, King of Heaven,
> New clothes like these,
> Do thou keep all nasty creatures
> Out of this frieze.
> He'll direct us, He'll defend us,
> If Him we please,
> Lord, keep all nasty creatures
> Out of this frieze.

Her masterpiece is *The Interior Castle*, a guide to spiritual perfection which presents the soul as a castle containing seven concentric dwelling places, the center of which is the dwelling place of God. Teresa explains that to reach the center one must pass through each of the intermediate stages. It is a difficult book, made more so by Teresa's complex and involved manner of thinking: Once an idea possessed her she wrote it down; and if another intruded before the first was completed she inserted it, so that at times the paragraphs become parentheses within parentheses. Teresa's 19th century daughter, St. Therese of Lisieux, admits that she finds her Mother's great theological work stiff going. But theologians, then and now, have revelled in it; and once the wrinkles in the rhetoric have been ironed out it is remarkably clear and illuminating.

William Herr, in his essay on St. Teresa in *Catholic Thinkers in the Clear*, provides one of the best summaries of the book available. For those interested in reading the original it might serve both as an introduction and a valuable guide.

Her spiritual director, who had told her to write the book, was so impressed with it that he could not resist showing it to a few special friends. The Princess of Eboli heard about it and demanded a copy so that she could read "and benefit by it." The princess was not one to keep confidences; and soon Teresa's "revelations," exaggerated and embroidered for common consumption, came to the notice of the Inquisition.

Teresa was not afraid of the Inquisition. In fact, when her first writings—her *Life* and the *Way of Perfection*—appeared, and some theologians told her they feared the Holy Office might send for her, she was very much interested. She said that if there was anything in her work that was wrong or needed elucidation, she would like to go at once and present herself before the Grand Inquisitor. Her *Interior Castle* eventually did come before the Holy Office; and after both it and her life had been examined she was cleared of all charges and declared orthodox, although she was warned to limit her teaching in the future. Her answer—that she had never taught any but her sisters, for whom as their superior she was responsible—was accepted, although today it sounds more naive than Teresa usually was, for she certainly knew the impact her writings had on those outside the boundaries of the reformed Carmel.

In the meantime all was not running smoothly in some of the convents. Benefactors made demands regarding postulants to the order, not all of whom were suitable. Some of the prioresses, allowed to run their houses their own way while Teresa was spending increasing time away from them because of her age and uncertain health, became little dictators, either demanding mortifications the sensible Teresa could not condone or permitting luxuries and dispensations from the Rule.

She continued to guide the sisters, warning them that "We must not show ourselves to be striving after spiritual consolations; come what may, the great thing to do is for us to embrace the Cross." This is the hard core of St. Teresa's spiritual strength.

She was worried about the members of her family, although she was glad to use the money her brother brought back from America for her foundation expenses. But by 1582 it was clear that she was in physical decline; and when she arrived at Alba de Tormes, the religious house she had opened in 1571, it was obvious she would travel no further. She knew she had to make only one more journey, and she had no apprehensions. "My Lord," she exclaimed, "it is time to set out; may the journey be propitious, and may Thy will be done."

Her last days were painful ones, and she spent them in almost continual prayer. At the end she was heard to whisper, "A contrite and humble heart, O God, you will not despise;" and a few moments later, with a warm smile, "I die a daughter of the church." Her death came on October 4, 1582; and with her passed one of the warmest, wittiest, most courageous women of any age, an amazingly modern woman whose spirituality was tempered by an unflinching realism.

From her we learn what God expects of each of us. She says, "Once when I was wishing I could do something in Our Lord's service, I considered how little I could do to serve Him; and I said to myself, 'Why, Lord, dost thou desire my works?' He answered, 'to see thy good will.' And that is all he asks of us."

Teresa was canonized in 1622; and in 1970, together with Catherine of Siena, was made a doctor of the church, the only two women in that august company.

St. Margaret Clitheroe
c1556-1586

THE city of York is a fascinating blend of the contemporary and the old. The new University of York resembles any number of mid-western state universities in the United States; and one American professor, commenting on the fact to a faculty member of the British university, was surprised to learn that York University had, in fact, been planned and built only after a committee had studied universities in America, adapting what seemed practical to their own situation.

The past is magnificently represented by York Minster, one of the more beautiful cathedrals in a country famous for the variety and glory of these buildings. Yorkshiremen take pride in their Minster, and during World War II the exquisite Seven Sisters window was removed and buried to preserve it from the bombings which that industrial town suffered repeatedly. And if one is fascinated by the past, there is the ancient wall encircling what used to be the limits of York city, and which was saved from demolition by a vote not too many decades ago.

But for the Catholic pilgrim the place which draws like a magnet is none of these, but the little timbered home, now a shrine, at No. 36, the Shambles, the narrow medieval street where the butchers used to ply their trade. It was there that Margaret Clitheroe, the young Elizabethan martyr, lived above the shop her husband owned, the house where she hid proscribed priests. And it was for this crime that she was put to death under Elizabeth in 1586.

Hers was a complex society in which we meet something of modern dichotomies, a society which demonstrated the skill with which a strong political party can throw confusion over the issue which we still face today: the usurpation by the state of the rights of God.

Among the martyrs of her century she has many points of resemblance and of contrast with St. Thomas More. Both were, primarily, family martyrs, who were devoted to partners in marriage who did not understand their uncompromising stands and attached to their children, but who placed the love of God over intense family love. Both had gaiety and courage, wit and charity. Both possessed shrewdness in worldly affairs, and Margaret's recorded utterances at her trial resemble More's in nobility of phrase and unwavering steadfastness. Her gaiety and courage, and the fact that she was the mother of a young family, add poignancy to her story.

The dates of Margaret's life are not quite certain, but two we definitely know. She was married on July 15, 1571; and she died on March 25, 1586, a day which was Lady Day in spring according to the old calendar and Good Friday by the new. She had been a Catholic twelve years, and had a boy of fourteen.

Her childhood was brief in an age when a girl often

married at fifteen. From all accounts they were happy years, even though it was a period when for the average citizen things religious were at their most confused. Margaret was about two years old when Elizabeth came to the throne, and about three when the new religion was imposed. Her mother had no more education than was usual for women at that time; her father, Thomas Middleton, was an invalid, Catholic by habit rather than by conviction; and their vicar had a foot in each camp. As a result, the influences of her earliest years were neither strongly Catholic nor Protestant; but as York and the whole north of England slowly changed loyalties it is certain that the famous York mystery plays were continued at Corpus Christi, and that Margaret was influenced by the story of Christ's passion as it was enacted before her.

Her father, a well-to-do chandler, conformed at least outwardly to the new laws; and as a result he prospered. He was made a member of the Common Council of York; and in 1564, when Margaret was probably eleven, he was made one of the two sheriffs of the city. Later in the year he was so ill that he had to be excused from his duties. In 1567, when Margaret was 14, he died. Four months after her father's death her mother married again, to a man without wealth or standing who owed his admission into the inner circle of York entirely to his marriage to her. Henry May did very well with his wife behind him. He became alderman, and at last Lord Mayor of York—at the very time his stepdaughter came to trial.

But Margaret apparently liked her stepfather, for when her first baby was born she named him Henry.

She had received a good training in keeping a house, which in her day meant far more than it does now. She had to master baking bread and brewing ale, and also how to supervise the weavers, tailers, and others who came to the house to work, as well as the women servants who would help in the house and shop. She was also expected to be able to run her husband's business while he was away.

Her innkeeper step-father arranged her marriage to John Clitheroe, a widower with two children. She left her home in Davygate, where she had been born, and went to live in her husband's house in the butchers' quarter of York, the Shambles; for at that time men practising the same trade lived in the same part of town. She was a girl of eighteen, beautiful, with a mass of light brown hair and a clear skin; her biographer does not mention the color of her eyes. But the most attractive feature of the young woman was her vivacity, a merriment which hid the depths of her character. As she had a good dowry, her husband, John, was delighted with his girl-wife.

He was a Protestant and one of the wealthiest citizens in York, a fact attested to by the town records which show he was assessed for poor relief at the highest rate. John Clitheroe was a man who loved company and delighted in taking his charming wife to banquets —sometimes private parties in a neighbor's house, sometimes ceremonial dinners of the butchers' company. And since the citizens of York led a very active social life, the young couple would be invited to the feasts at the Common Hall, especially when Margaret's step-father became Lord Mayor. Margaret was naturally a pleasure-loving Elizabethan, and John Clitheroe can be forgiven for thinking she was totally involved in the enjoyment of the good things of this world.

But there were depths to her character; and while we will never know what particular incident touched her, it is probable she saw Thomas Percy, Earl of Northumberland, beheaded. At the time of his execution he said, "If I had 1000 lives I would give them up for the Catholic faith." Who it was that instructed Margaret and eventually received her into the church it is impossible to say; but he was almost certainly an old, or Marian, priest, with faculties to absolve those who returned to the faith. The date of her reconciliation was two or three years at the most after her marriage: that would be in 1573 or 1574. In March, 1586, she said she had been a Catholic for twelve years. It is also possible that one of her husband's brothers was influential in her conversion; both of them were Catholic, and one was a priest.

In our day, when the major crisis regarding the Mass for Catholics is whether they like the service in the vernacular or have nostalgic preference for the old Latin celebration, whether they like a silent Mass or enjoy the varied and new liturgies, whether they prefer accompaniment by the guitar or the organ, it is difficult to conceive of attendance at Mass as a life-threatening action. But so it became in Margaret Clitheroe's day, when England was under interdict and the queen, like her father before her, had been excommunicated for claiming to be the head of the church. When Elizabeth came to the throne a law had been passed forbidding the mass and ordering the whole population to attend the queen's service in English in the parish churches.

Margaret's conversion brought her into contact with a flourishing underground community of Catholics. Whether or not her husband realized the situation clearly, he certainly was aware that his wife was not attending the new church, for he paid the fine for non-attendance—but then, since he was not a particularly religious man, he paid for his own absence as well; and he was no Roman Catholic. Apparently he obligingly turned his back on whatever his wife was up to, but this did not really comfort her. Her frank nature found concealment abhorrent, especially between husband and wife. She tried to make up to him by being as good a wife as she could be; and that she succeeded is apparent in the record, when John Clitheroe said he could wish for no better wife, were it not for two faults: she fasted too much, and would not go with him to church.

John Clitheroe was not a bad sort of man, but he had no intention of bringing unpleasantness on himself for the sake of religion. An open Catholic who refused to go to the national church was fined a shilling for every absence. This would come to between $150 and $200 a year, making being a Catholic a dangerous and expensive luxury. In addition, all public office was closed to Catholics. John Clitheroe accepted office as a chamberlain, and declared publicly that he accepted the queen's supremacy in religion. But he made things as easy as he could for his wife. He paid her fines, gave her money for her many works of charity, and was careful to know nothing about the priests who came to his house to say Mass.

It was a comfortable marriage, although they had their "tiffs." Margaret admitted "to such small matters as are commonly incident to husband and wife," and it is possible that her own temper was a quick one. One of the things about which they differed was the shop. John Clitheroe was both a wholesale butcher and retailer; and since the wholesale business brought in a sufficient income, Margaret wished to give up the shop. She didn't like being known as the wealthy Clitheroes. But she had to content herself with finding out early in the morning before the shop opened what other butchers were charging in order to charge the same. She was not interested in attracting business by competition, especially since they were living comfortably enough and in no real need, as some of their competitors might well be.

She was a warm and devoted mother, loving her children intensely but teaching them lessons in self-sacrifice and integrity. What is remarkable is that not one of her children was under her care after the age of twelve. Henry was 14 when she died, but had been sent abroad to school two years earlier. Anne was 12 and William perhaps nine or ten at the time of her death. Nor had Margaret had them in her care even for the whole of those short years: she had been separated from them by her imprisonments, once for two years. After her death efforts were made to turn William and Anne against their mother's religion. But it was all in vain. Margaret remained for their whole lives the strongest influence over her children. They remained true to her teaching all their days. This hold on her children was one of Margaret's outstanding feats.

As for their religion, it was shown them not as a duty but a privilege. What fortunate children they were to have our blessed Lord himself so often in their own home! And if they had to pay for this sometimes by having to go without their mother because she had been hauled off to prison, it taught them to turn for help directly to Our Lord and his holy Mother. She made the faith so attractive that her son, Henry, became a priest, as did her step-son William; and her daughter, Anne, became a nun. Her step-son Thomas died a confessor for the faith after several years imprisonment.

To Margaret, forced to shut her husband out from the joy at the core of her life, it must have been the deepest comfort to bring her children in. Her house was one of the chief Mass centers of York, and her children were admitted to all that was afoot. It was natural they should know how their tutor could slip out of the window of their attic schoolroom and escape through the house next door. But they knew much more than that. They knew the secret of the cupboard where the vestments were kept, and the altar breads. They knew, too, the priest's hole in their own house, and another at a distance.

Margaret herself went to confession and usually to communion every Wednesday and Sunday. She arranged for Mass to be said in her home when possible, but usually in a neighboring building from which a priest might escape more easily. It was a dangerous business; but the attack on the Mass made devout Catholics like Margaret more devoted, and deeply aware of their share in the redemptive sufferings and sacrifice of Christ.

When the worst of the Penal Acts were passed, the terrible statutes of 1585 under which most of the martyrs suffered, a timid neighbor came and warned Margaret to be more careful. Since harboring a priest was now treason and felony, he suggested that she discontinue receiving priests and allowing the Mass to be said on her premises. He added that it was most unwise and imprudent to know everything that was going on.

He left Margaret worried, but she also was convinced that nothing ought to be preferred to obedience to God. She told her advisor that Christ had said at the Last Supper, "Do this in memory of me;" and she had no intention of not remembering him.

History has been ambivalent in its evaluation of Elizabeth: she is "good Queen Bess," during whose reign England became a great and cultured nation; but she is also remembered for the bloody persecution which took place while she was on the throne. In justice to Elizabeth it should be noted that she, herself, was content with outward conformity: on one occasion she stated clearly and emphatically that she desired to "open no windows into men's souls, remitting that to the supreme and singular authority of Almighty God, who is the only searcher of hearts." Had York not been so far from London (a journey in those days of two to three days), it is doubtful that Margaret Clitheroe would have been put to death.

Only three women in the whole reign of Elizabeth

were called upon to lay down their lives, according to Margaret Monro; but the number who died in prison has never been counted. All faced the accusation of disloyalty, a particular anguish since their loyalty to the faith cut through their dearest human loyalties. It was this factor in their suffering, as it was for Margaret, which made their ordeal more unbearable.

The pressures became greater on those who did not attend the Queen's service, and Margaret was first jailed in August, 1577. When she was released she set up a safer Mass center in the house next to hers. She was jailed again twice for non-attendance, after which she arranged for her son Henry to be sent abroad to study.

In March of 1586, the Council of the North, members of which were selected for their persecuting spirit, came to York; and one of its first acts was to send for John Clitheroe to explain the absence of his son. While her husband was before the council the sheriff of York arrived to search the house. Everything points to her stepfather as responsible for the raid, for it was unthinkable that the step-daughter of the Lord Mayor should be an embarrassment to him. It is easy to imagine Margaret's horror when she realized who had sent the council to her home.

Father Mush, her first biographer, was nearly caught; but he got safely away. She and her servants were detained downstairs while the upper floors were searched. No noise warned those upstairs, and the first the tutor knew was when the door of the schoolroom was opened and closed again. He locked the door and skipped out through a window, and when the searchers burst open the door they found nothing but a group of children.

Margaret was not afraid of the servants' betraying her, for they were deeply attached to her. She shared the roughest work in the house with them and she asked nothing of her maids that she was unwilling to do with them.

She had no worries about her children either, and had it only been the little Clitheroes the searchers might not have gained much. They and the neighbor children were fearless, and from the time when Margaret had gathered them to share the chance of a Catholic schooling they had been alerted to the dangers of such a possibility. But there was a little 14-year-old boy who had not been in England for long; his father was English and his mother Flemish. He had heard about the suffering of the martyrs in England, and now the terror was before him. The men of the council recognized which of the children would break, and threatened the frightened youngster with a flogging. He broke down and showed them all they wanted to know: where Mass was said, where the vestments and altar breads were kept. He told them everything he knew; and, as was revealed later, things he did not know. At any rate, it was more than the pursuivants had dreamed of obtaining.

Margaret was arrested, as were her husband and children; all were confined separately. Margaret was never allowed to see her children again. Anne was placed in a conformer's home and treated with great harshness to make her go to church. (A particularly brutal trick was played on her: after Margaret's death

Anne was told she could save her mother's life if she would go to church and hear a sermon. She yielded once, but when she realized the cruel deceit she never again gave in.)

Margaret was the first woman accused under the new law of 1585, which imposed the death penalty. When she was brought before the court she was merry and smiling. Her attitude infuriated her accusers; and she was returned to prison on March 10, where she was alone for two days. Then on Saturday they arrested a friend of Margaret's, Anne Tesch. The council sent for the Flemish boy to ask if he recognized her as one who had attended Mass in Margaret's house, but the boy to their disappointment did not. Anne Tesch was sent to join Margaret in prison in spite of this; and the two were delighted to be together, making fun of the inconveniences of their cell, "no spoons, broken cups and plates." The interview with her husband was more sobering. It took place in the presence of the jailer and was the last time they were allowed to be together. Father Mush's biography quotes her as saying, "Know you that I love him next to God in this world. If I have offended my husband in anything but my conscience in my religious duty, I ask God's and his forgiveness."

Margaret's school of holiness was prison. It was here that she had leisure for God, and, as she said, for "giving me a chance for the getting of those virtues which I perceive to be wanting in me." It is characteristic that she should have thrown herself into gaining virtues rather than uprooting faults.

Back in court her indictment was read: that she had "harboured and maintained Jesuits and seminary priests, traitors to the queen's majesty and her laws," and that she had heard Mass. Judge Clinch, who did not want to see her die, asked, "Margaret Clitheroe, are you guilty of this indictment or no?" She answered with a smile, "I know of no offence whereof I should confess myself guilty." Judge Clinch's concern was to be relieved of responsibility for her death, so he passed over her reply and asked, "How will you be tried?"

At this point Margaret sprang her surprise. She replied, "Having done no offence, I need no trial. But if you say I have offended and must be tried I will be tried by none but God and your own conscience."

This was exactly what Clinch wished to avoid; his conscience revolted against the whole business. So he argued with her for a time, saying, "We sit here to see justice done, and therefore you must be tried by the jury." He badly wanted twelve men to share his blame; Margaret as badly wanted to restrict it to one man, since she knew she stood no chance of acquittal.

Clinch continued, "In whom do you believe?"

Margaret answered, "I believe in God."

"In what God?" asked the judge.

"I believe in God the Father, in God the Son, and God the Holy Ghost; in these three persons I fully believe, and that by the passion, death and merits of Christ Jesu I must be saved."

Huddleston provided the most shocking touch in all this travesty of justice. He called out from the bench, "It is not for religion that thou harborest priests, but for harlotry." But even the court rejected this; and the murmurs of disapproval must have been of some slight comfort to Margaret, for such an accusation made no impression on those in the courtroom who knew her. She was taken back to prison, but to a much worse prison built on the bridge over the river Ouse.

As the law stood, any prisoner who refused to plead was sentenced to what was called the *peine forte et dure,* which meant the accused was laid naked on the stone floor of an underground cell; a door was placed over him; and weights were piled on the door so that life was literally pressed out of the victim.

On March 15 she was taken back to the Guild Hall. Judge Clinch began by saying, "We see no reason why you should refuse to be cooperative; there be but small witness against you."

Margaret went straight to the heart of the matter, saying, "You have no witness against me but a child, who with an apple and a rod you may make say what you will." She was reminded of the much more dangerous evidence that she had entertained priests in her home, and that "things of the Mass" had been found there. At this point Clinch returned to the question, "Will you put yourself to the jury, yes or no?" She answered again, but with a direct hit at the entire procedure, "I refer my cause to God and your own conscience."

At this moment Wiggington, a Puritan preacher, shouted, "My lord, take heed what you do. You sit here to do justice; this woman's case touches life and death; you ought not, either by God's law or man's, to judge her to die upon the slender evidence of a boy. . . . Therefore, my lord, this is serious business."

Clinch answered, "I may do it by law."

Wiggington asked, "By what law?"

St. Margaret Clitheroe

Clinch answered defiantly, "By the Queen's law."

"That may well be," said the Puritan, "but you cannot do it by God's law." The judge interrupted by addressing himself directly to Margaret, "If you will not put yourself to the jury, your judgment must be *forte et dure.*"

Margaret heard the sentence and then said quietly, "If this judgment be according to your conscience I beg God to send you a better judgment before Him." She had chosen the death that would most spare others.

For all her apparent calm Margaret had had a shock: she had not expected that she would be stripped naked, and this troubled her more than the death itself. Back at the prison she dealt with it practically. Obtaining a length of linen and some tape, she made a loose garment open down the back with long sleeves ending in tapes so that her hands might be bound.

When her husband heard of her condemnation "he fared like a man out of his wits, and wept so vehemently that blood gushed out of his nose. 'Alas, will they kill my wife? Let them take all I have and save her, for she is the best wife in all England, and the best Catholic also.'" Her husband was ordered out of the city for ten days, and her friends knew this was the indication that the sentence was to be carried out.

During those ten days she was sometimes overwhelmed with fear; but most of the time she was her usual self, cheerful, practical, self-possessed, and above all, resolute. From the day of her condemnation she ate little; some soup, rye bread, and small ale, which she took only once a day. After she was told that in two days she was to die she took no further food, but made her final arrangements very quietly, sending her bonnet-like headdress to her husband, her shoes and stockings to little Anne. The little girl took the hint, and the convent annals in France say of her, "Sister Anne Clitheroe followed well her holy mother's virtuous footsteps."

A fellow prisoner, Mrs. Yoward, reported that at midnight the night before her execution Margaret got up, dressed herself in the long linen robe, and in the cold of the March night knelt praying for several hours. About three in the morning she went over to the fireplace and lay down on her back for about a quarter of an hour. Was she rehearsing her death? Mrs. Yoward heard her whisper, "Jesus, Jesus, be to me Jesus" a number of times.

In the morning when the sheriffs came they found her ready. At the Toll Booth she knelt down and prayed aloud for the church, the pope and cardinals, and for all Christian rulers, especially for Elizabeth, Queen of England . . . "for I wish as much good to her Majesty's soul as to my own."

At the place of execution women removed her clothing and put on her the long linen robe. "Then very quietly she lay down on the floor, her hands folded in prayer. A sharp stone the size of a man's fist was placed under her back, a door was laid over her . . . her hands bound to two stakes in the floor so that she lay with arms outstretched in the form of a cross."

Four hired beggars began to lay the weights upon the door. As she felt them she was heard to say, "Jesu, Jesu, have mercy on me." After that, no further sound was heard save the terrible crash of the weights, "700 or

St. Margaret Clitheroe

800 weight at the least." She was about a quarter of an hour dying, and the watchers stood round waiting while a pool of blood formed on the floor. The sheriffs left the body there for six hours; they then buried it after dark in some waste ground where they hoped it would never be found, or at least not identified.

Six weeks later some Catholics succeeded in locating it. They reported the body was incorrupt, although terribly mangled. Where it was then buried was a secret so carefully guarded that it was lost.

For us 400 years later her martyrdom has a special significance, steadfast as she was in a swirling sea of opposition and of confusing issues. She must have been shaken in mind and body many times, especially in the terrible final ten days. But like Joan of Arc, her very weakness was her strength, for it forced her to put all her trust in God. Bishop Challoner points to her exquisite concern for the consciences of others, which induced her not to plead "that she might not bring others into danger by her conviction, or be accessory to the jurymen's sins in condemning the innocent."

She was canonized on October 25, 1970, by Pope Paul VI as one of the English martyrs; and now in Yorkshire, as throughout the world, mothers in difficulty turn to her for help, saying simply, "St. Margaret Clitheroe, pray for me."

Elizabeth Seton
1774–1821

ELIZABETH Anne Bayley Seton, the first native-born American saint (Mother Cabrini and Bishop John Neumann were both naturalized citizens), was a significantly appropriate woman to be so honored. She was born before the United States separated from England and was a child during the American Revolution. The list of her friends and relatives reads like a *Who's Who* of the early Republic, although her father was staff surgeon to Admiral Lord Howe of the British navy. Two 20th-century presidents, Theodore and Franklin Delano Roosevelt, are branches on her family tree. Like the majority of United States citizens, she came from mixed ancestry: some of her forebears immigrated from England; but her mother's grandparents were French Huguenots who sought religious freedom in the New World as early as 1686, and at the beginning of the 18th century they owned a lion's share of what is today New Rochelle, New York. The fact of her canonization the year before the United States celebrated its bi-centennial is significant: she proves that while Roman Catholicism was the religion of the minority, some distinguished citizens belonged to the church; and Elizabeth Bayley Seton is also evidence that sanctity existed from the beginning of our country.

She was an American who lived during and was influenced by the early history about which we read. Her fortune fluctuated with that of the nation. Her two sons were in the United States Navy, a fact commemorated annually the first Sunday of October when the United States Naval Academy Catholic Midshipmen Chapel Choir sings the liturgy at the Elizabeth Seton shrine chapel in Emmitsburg.

Elizabeth Bayley was born in New York City on August 28, 1774, the second daughter of Doctor Richard Bayley and Catherine Charlton. There are no records of her baptism, since Trinity church, where it may have been performed, lost its records in the fire of 1776. Her mother died when Elizabeth was only three years old; but Elizabeth remembered her gentle, loving personality all her life. Doctor Bayley remarried a little over a year later to Charlotte Amelia Barclay, a member of one of New York's best-known families.

The second marriage was not a happy one, although Doctor Bayley and his wife had six children. Elizabeth's stepmother was as kind as her nature allowed to the three children of her husband's first marriage, but she had little time to spend with them. Doctor Bayley was a dedicated physician; and as professor at King's College, now Columbia University, his days were too crowded to allow him much leisure for his growing family—although he was devoted to them, especially to Elizabeth, his acknowledged favorite.

On her seventh birthday her father gave her and her

sister Mary a journal; and explained to the little girls its purpose, helping and showing them how to keep them. It was a practice Elizabeth was to continue with short lapses for the rest of her life, one which reveals her development of mind and spirit; for the journal is not primarily a record of events, but of her inner contemplation of them.

Two items recur continually, an indication that even in her childhood the focus of her soul included references to her dead mother and simple but poignant personal prayers to God. On August 1, for example, in a vague reference to a domestic crisis in which she and her sister Mary and her little slave boy, Brenner, were involved, she notes, "'The patient man is better than he who taketh cities.' I am glad father came home in time. I am grateful to our dear Savior; I read the 14th chapter of St. Matthew."

This balance of record, reflection and prayer was to continue to be the pattern in her Journal until the end of her life, with prayer becoming more and more prominent.

Elizabeth received the usual education given daughters of the upper-class at that time: she was taught music and sewing, and played the harpsichord with skill. She also became an accomplished horsewoman; and, of course, learned how to dance. She had learned to speak French while her mother was alive; and both she and Mary remained bi-lingual all their lives, their competence increased by a tutor and such reading as they themselves undertook. In later years Elizabeth would remark that she regretted the hours she spent reading Rousseau; but since everyone around her was fascinated by the French author, it would have been unusual had she not been attracted also.

Doctor Bayley was aware of his wife's resentment of Elizabeth, and decided she would develop with less strain away from home. When she was eight years old she was sent to her Aunt Molly, who conducted a small school in her home. It was a happy resolution to a difficult situation; and while Elizabeth missed her father and sister Mary, she had other children with whom she could play and a devoted aunt who watched over the little girl with real affection. Summers she spent with her step-mother's sister, Catherine Barclay, whose summer home on the Hudson was one of the finest in the area.

Elizabeth had never lived in such a large house as the Van Cortlandt's; but she quickly adapted, and made the most of the spacious grounds with their beautiful gardens. Another little cousin, Marta Van Cortlandt, was invited to be a companion to Elizabeth; and the two little girls spent the long summer days enjoying the freedom from books. Catherine Barclay even arranged a "children's ball" one summer to which the children of neighboring estates were invited. She initiated her two small nieces in the responsibilities of being a gracious hostess.

Elizabeth's concern for the poor, unusual in so young a child, saw an outlet in personal service and in the founding of the Elizabeth Bayley Society for Helping the Poor, which she organized at Aunt Molly's school.

Her friends who joined her named the club for the foundress, much to Elizabeth's distress; but her aunt convinced her the name was nothing: it was the works the group did which would have value with God. According to Elizabeth's journal it was Aunt Molly who suggested they write the names of five poor families on different slips of paper and each girl draw one for the year.

When Elizabeth was 14 years old, she and her sister Mary were invited to spend some time at the home of the Setons, friends of her father. The Setons were well-to-do, sharing a mercantile business with Mr. Maitland. Although the Revolutionary War had brought changes to the merchant class, William Seton retained the bulk of his holdings and became the cashier of the newly organized Bank of New York. When Alexander Hamilton became Secretary of the Treasury, the senior Seton became involved in Hamilton's plans for the financial security of the federal government.

While a guest in their home Elizabeth met the eldest son, William Magee Seton, and they were mutually attracted. The young man had been prepared to become his father's successor in the business. He had been educated in England; and the year of Elizabeth's visit he was sent abroad to visit various businesses and to study finance at first hand in the business of the Italian financiers Filipo and Antonio Filicchi in Leghorn, Italy. During the years of his absence Elizabeth matured from the adolescent who was a guest in his home to a beautiful and accomplished young woman.

Her sister Mary, married young Doctor Post, her father's assistant. Elizabeth's father had returned to England for additional conferences with the doctors there; and Elizabeth spent part of the time on Staten

Island with her mother's relatives, the Dongans, and much of her time with her newly married sister. New York after the war was a busy social center. The Bayleys and Posts were welcome everywhere to evenings of music and dancing, and Elizabeth soon became famous as the most beautiful young woman in the exclusive circle in which she moved. Her godmother, Mrs. Startin, introduced her officially to society; and promised to leave her not inconsiderable fortune to Elizabeth and Mary.

Elizabeth had promised William Seton that she would correspond with him, and to her a promise was sacred. When he returned he discovered the young woman to whom he had been sending amusing comments on Italian life had matured into a beauty. Within a brief time he had gone through the preliminaries of 18th century society: asking her father for permission to marry her, telling his own family of his plans, and receiving their enthusiastic approval. Finally he made the formal proposal to Elizabeth herself. It was an unusual marriage for that time, for William and Elizabeth had married for love and not for fortune. The pictures of the young couple show a delicate but striking young man and a slight, beautiful girl of nineteen.

In addition to the joy her love for her husband gave her, she relaxed for the first time in a home she could call her own on 27 Wall Street. Although she was to live there only four years, it remained in her memory a place of great happiness: her first daughter, Anna Maria, was born there on May 3, 1795. Her first son, William, who was to hold a special place in her heart until her death, was born the following year, November 25, 1796; and the third, another boy named Richard Bayley, arrived on July 20, 1798.

But the untroubled early years came to an abrupt halt with the death of William's father. Of the seven youngest children only Rebecca, 18, was old enough to accept responsibility; so William and Elizabeth were forced to take in the six younger children, the burden of which, of course, fell upon Elizabeth, herself scarcely more than a girl. Rebecca proved a real blessing during this time of readjustment in family life; for although her health was a source of anxiety, she was willing to do more than her share in the care of the children and housekeeping, leaving her brother and Elizabeth free to work on trying to bring order into what was to prove to be a series of disasters.

The Setons' financial situation became more and more critical. Had his father lived, the firm might have withstood the pressures of Britain's undeclared war with France, which brought about the confiscation of Seton ships and cargo; but young William was still a novice in financial affairs, and was unable as head of the firm to exert the strong pressure that was needed. In December of 1799 the London half of the firm, the Maitlands, stopped payments on the British debts. An accountant, Garrett Killett, came to take an inventory of stock; William was forced to hand over the key to the Mill Street counting house and to admit bankruptcy. The young Setons sold their home in New York with its furnishings, a futile effort to pay their creditors. Not only did their fortune seem to melt away, but the debts did not appear to diminish.

Elizabeth wrote in her journal, "It would never do to let our hearts and fortunes sink at the same time. What, God, do you ask of me?"

Her love of nature, attention to the needs of her family, and spiritual bent helped her keep her peace and serenity in the shock of failure. She was deeply aware that God was the basis of her peace, and wrote, "Preserve me in this heavenly peace; let me continue to rest in Thee, and adore Thee, my Father, Friend, and never-failing support."

Fortunately at this time her relationship with her public-spirited father continued to be close. He offered Elizabeth, who was expecting her fourth child, the summer house on Staten Island near the hospital he had persuaded the city to build. The family had hardly settled into their new home when immigrants arriving in New York harbor brought an epidemic of yellow fever which spread like fire through the city. Her father, as the newly appointed health commissioner, tried to enforce quarantine laws. Working night and day with a rapidly diminishing corps of assistants, he eventually fell victim himself. On August 11 he came home from his morning rounds with a raging fever; by afternoon he was delirious. Elizabeth sent the children to her sister, Mary, and herself cared for her father. Six days later, his hand in hers, he said quietly, "The love of God is over us all," and then, "Christ, have mercy on me;" and in perfect peace died. She wrote her friend, Julia Scott, "Surely the next blessing in our future existence to that of being near the Source of Perfection will be the enjoyment of each other's company without dread of interruption."

St. Elizabeth Anne Seton

Trials once begun seemed to increase for Elizabeth. Scarcely had she buried her father when the doctors informed her and William of the serious threat to his health from the "white plague," consumption. A sea voyage and the opportunity to convalesce in a warmer climate seemed the only chance of survival. William's friends, the Filicchi brothers, invited them to come and if possible to bring the children. After discussing all possibilities, Elizabeth and William decided that financially they could not afford to take the five children; and the oldest, little Anna Maria, should be the one to accompany her parents. One-year old Rebecca would move to Elizabeth's sister, Mary, and the other three would live with William's sister, Rebecca, and Elizabeth Sadler.

They booked passage on *The Shepherdess*, leaving relatives and friends in October, 1803. Six weeks later, November 19, after a stormy voyage, the ship finally dropped anchor at the pier in Leghorn. Elizabeth flew to the deck to greet her half-brother Carleton Bayley, who had come out to meet them with the Filicchi brothers. In her joy at seeing him Elizabeth did not at first notice that Carleton made no motion to approach her. Only when a guard ordered, "Don't touch" did she realize that all was not well. *The Shepherdess* was from New York, where fever was raging; and because the vessel lacked a bill of health, it would have to go into quarantine. The Leghorn quarantine was several miles from the city on a canal. The Setons were rowed out to the dungeon-like building, taking with them only the barest necessities.

Several days later the captain and guards brought a

bed for William, who had been forced to sleep on the damp, cold stones until then. The Filicchis sent curtains to prevent a draft, and benches for Elizabeth and Anna Maria. They also provided a servant, Luigi, to take some of the burden of William's care from Elizabeth; and daily sent food which William, now a dying man, consistently refused. The quarantine was to last thirty days; but a dispensation was given them, since they had spent several weeks at sea. They were told they would be released on December 19, and would spend Christmas in Pisa. It was a dreadful time. Elizabeth watched her husband's health deteriorate by the day, with fever, chills, weakness and depression increasing, while the only medication she had was some Iceland moss and opium, which William took listlessly and obviously without hope.

To Elizabeth the days were as years. Little Anna Maria developed a severe chest pain, and Elizabeth herself was exhausted. But the days in the Lazaretto were days of spiritual grace for William. His thoughts were almost constantly on heaven, and he told Elizabeth that whether he lived or died he would consider the time blessed.

Eventually quarantine was lifted on December 19; and the Setons did go to Pisa, carried there by the waiting coach of the Filicchis. William was delighted to be released from the confinement and discomfort of the Lazaretto; he felt so improved that he insisted on taking rides in the carriage. On Christmas Eve, however, when he returned from his ride he had to be carried to bed. It was the end. For two days he was in and out of consciousness; and on the morning of

St. Elizabeth Anne Seton

December 27, reaching out his arms to Elizabeth, he said, "You promised you would go," and died.

In spite of the kindness of the Filicchis, the next days were a nightmare for Elizabeth: the arrangements for William's funeral in the Protestant cemetery in Leghorn, the sympathy of her friends while her family was miles away, the sad moment when she had told Anna Maria that they must together thank God that Papa's frightful sufferings were over. She wrote in her journal, "It is not necessary to dwell on the mercy and consoling presence of my dear Lord, for no mortal strength could support what I have experienced." Over and over she repeated, "My God, you are my God, and so I am alone in the world with you and my little ones, but you are my Father, and doubly theirs."

Elizabeth planned to return to the United States as soon as it could be arranged; but the day they were to leave, Anna Maria developed a high fever which was diagnosed as scarlet fever. It was not until three weeks later that Elizabeth was sure she might not possibly leave two graves behind instead of one.

The time, however, she was to recall later, was a special blessing. It was then she became interested in Catholicism as she saw it lived, not only by the Filicchis and their friends, but by the people she saw praying in the churches she visited, as the Filicchis took her to Florence and through the surrounding countryside. Philip gave her a copy of St. Francis de Sales' *Introduction to the Devout Life,* and she was moved by the procession of the Blessed Sacrament which passed her window. She thought, "How happy I would be to find God in the chapel, in the Sacrament."

Finally she and Anna Maria were able to leave. The Filicchi family all rose at four o'clock, and Elizabeth attended her last Mass there in the family chapel. Whether or not she was ready to become a Catholic at that time we have no way of knowing, but there is an entry in her journal for that day which would seem to suggest she was. "Last Mass at Leghorn at four in the morning; lost in the indescribable reverence and impressions kneeling in a little confessional, did not perceive an ear was waiting for me until the priest came out to ask Mrs. Filicchi why I did not begin."

Elizabeth's friendship with the Filicchis was to span the ocean, and would endure for the rest of their lives. Antonio promised to look after her and the children financially, a promise he faithfully kept. Before they parted at the wharf Philip urged her to repeat Alexander Pope's words:

> If I am right, O teach my heart still in the right to stay
> If I am wrong, Thy grace impart to find the better way.

Antonio had business in the United States, so he arranged to travel with Mrs. Seton and Anna Maria on the *Pyomingo* on April 8, 1804. They arrived in New York harbor June 4 and were met by her fatherless children, her relatives, and friends. Her responsibility now was to make a home for her children; but as she confided to her friend, Julia Scott, William had died content that she and the children would be financially independent when his affairs were settled. But there was an even greater deficiency in their assets. They did have enough to rent a small home about a mile from town, and by living frugally she was convinced they could manage. She was now what our generation would call a single parent, and the worries about the children's proper education and physical care were constantly with her.

In addition, her formerly strong Anglican faith was unsettled, as she struggled, prayed, and yearned for spiritual peace. Her Protestant friends told her that her attraction to Catholicism was a temptation; and her former friend and pastor, John Hobart, argued with her and gave her tracts showing that the worship of the Catholic Church was idolatrous. Antonio Filicchi, concerned about his friend's confusion, appealed to Baltimore's Bishop John Carroll, stressing the salvation of six souls, the children's as well as the mother's. On August 20, 1804, Bishop Carroll wrote her and from then on took an active interest in the Seton family. Elizabeth's uncertainty continued, augmented by her brother-in-law's insistence that she was ill-advised. Since Wright Post was subsidizing part of her expenses, his displeasure was a serious one.

Elizabeth's was the conflict many sincere converts have, but her problem was increased by her responsibility for the welfare of her little family and the opinion of her friends and relatives concerning the church. St. Peter's, the only Catholic church in New York, consisted chiefly of immigrants whom the state constitution had effectively deprived of every opportunity to rise socially and economically. Joining it would mean Mrs. Seton would move from the respectable majority to the disreputable minority.

Mary Hester Valentine

After a year of interior struggle Elizabeth made the final decision to join the church, and made her profession of faith in the Roman Catholic Church on March 14, 1805. It meant a radical change not only in her spiritual life but in her relationship with friends and family, and an increase in economic insecurity. Her sister Mary, came to her help in August, when Elizabeth's financial situation reached a crisis, by bringing the whole family to live with her at Greenwich.

But being dependent was not to Mrs. Seton's liking, and she sought solutions for her difficulties. Finally in May she moved to a house near St. Peter's which was large enough to serve as a home for her family and a small school as well. The initial success when a few little girls came was short-lived, partly because of religious prejudice, but also, one must admit, because of the lack of business acumen on the part of the school's directors.

Antonio Felicchi again proved to be a valuable friend. He not only provided for the education of her two sons at Georgetown, with the cooperation of Bishop Carroll, but urged the bishop to visit Mrs. Seton to see what might be done to alleviate her situation.

Both Bishop Cheverus of Boston and Bishop Carroll became interested in Elizabeth through the urging of Antonio. Bishop Carroll himself came to New York, and, after a week of instruction and spiritual direction, confirmed her. After his return to Baltimore he consulted his friend, Rev. William DuBourg; and together they invited Mrs. Seton to Baltimore to open a school for girls. Father DuBourg made Mrs. Seton a definite offer of a grant of land near St. Mary's College, and agreed to put as many girls as Elizabeth could manage under her direction. Her own little girls would thus be taken care of; and she would be near her two sons, William and Richard.

Although neither she nor the bishop realized it, the move to Baltimore was the first step in the founding of the Sisters of Charity. The new school flourished; and by December of the first year Elizabeth had ten girls as boarders, as many as she could manage. The source of study was the usual one of the day, including music, drawing and literature; at the recommendation of the now Archbishop Carroll, several parents were encouraged to send their children to her to prepare them for their first Communion.

It soon became obvious that the little house on Paca street was too small, as more and more parents pleaded to have their daughters enrolled in the successful school. A plan was proposed to build a larger one on grounds near the Sulpician Fathers' seminary in Emmitsburg. Samuel Sutherland Cooper, a wealthy convert from Philadelphia who planned to enter the seminary, decided, after consultation with Father DuBourg, to dispose of his inheritance by giving it to help with the new school. He added a desire of his own which met with Elizabeth's immediate approval: there should also be a small school for the poor.

The founding of the religious community was almost a natural outgrowth of the move to Emmitsburg. Elizabeth herself was aware of the subtle shift in emphasis when she wrote, "I shall be at the head of a community which will live under the strictest rules of order and regularity, but I shall not give those laws, nor have any care of compelling others to fulfill them."

She wrote to another friend, "Mr. Cooper has given a handsome property for the establishment of those who may choose to lead a religious life. We will begin our novitiate in a beautiful country place in the mountains."

By January there were four candidates for the new community; and all wore habits similar to Mrs. Seton's mourning clothes, a black dress with a shoulder cape and a simple white cap. They moved to Emmitsburg in 1809, to a stone house which would be their home for their first year. It was not a comfortable situation: four rooms, one of which was a chapel, for 16 people.

The first years of the little community resembled those of many religious congregations: limited funds, physical hardships, and phenomenal growth. Elizabeth Seton faced a problem peculiar to her situation as head of a congregation which, like Topsy, "just growed," and to which, in spite of Archbishop Carroll's bestowing on her the title "Mother Seton" when she took private vows for one year, she was not initially fully committed. She wrote Catherine Dupleix in 1811, "I am free . . . and as mother of our darlings, must always be so, since by the law of the church I so much love, I could never take on obligations which interfere with my duties to them, except I had an independent provision and guardian for them--which the whole world could not supply to my judgment for a mother." She accepted responsibility for the young women who joined the community, but her primary concern was the welfare of her own five children.

St. Elizabeth Anne Seton

An additional problem was the fact that the official superiors of the sisters were men, Sulpician priests, some of whom did not understand the needs of sisters. Some of the priests resented the sisters' loyalty to previous spiritual leaders; and all drew up arbitrary rules based frequently on what they conceived as appropriate for religious women. Bishop Flaget, one of their strongest friends, discussed the possibility of their joining the Daughters of Charity of St. Vincent de Paul, and applied to the convent at Bordeaux for sisters to come to Emmitsburg to train the American women in the spirit and usage of the Rule of St. Vincent. Three French sisters were selected; but although the Rule reached Emmitsburg, the French sisters never arrived.

Actually this was a blessing, for the adaptations Mother Seton and her little group made were more compatable with the spirit of America than the French Rule would have been, and saved them from the accusation of being a foreign sisterhood, a serious one at that time.

Though frequently discouraged and confused about her duties over the years, she confided to Father Bruté, her confessor and later Bishop of Vincennes, Indiana, that she thought she did not part a minute of the day from Jesus. She fell asleep with him, and then woke to receive him in the Eucharist.

She had need of that union when the weak lungs which the children had inherited from their father began to betray the fatal symptoms. First Anna Maria contracted tuberculosis, and took vows as a Sister of Charity on her deathbed, March 12, 1812. Then the youngest, Rebecca, 11 years old, slipped on the ice while playing and injured her leg. In spite of the best medical care that could be given, the little girl remained unable to walk; and in 1815 a painful tumor developed on the injured leg. It was clear that the child was dying, and Elizabeth stayed with her as much as possible. On one occasion when she suggested to the child that they pray together, Rebecca replied, "Dearest mother, I am praying all the time." She died on November 3, 1816, at the age of 14.

Catherine, the remaining daughter, was the only one who outlived her mother. Her genes must have been a throw-back to some healthier ancestor, for she joined the Sisters of Mercy and lived to be 91 years old. Elizabeth's two sons, both of whom had served apprenticeships with the Filicchis in Italy, decided against going into business and entered the Navy instead.

Mother Seton's energies were free to devote to her community, now called the Sisters of Charity of St. Joseph; but she began to realize that her body was finally showing the effects of the years of strain—of her litany of deaths, as she called them. But exhausted as she was, she could still rouse herself when she felt the occasion demanded it. To Father John Hickey, assistant at Mount St. Mary's and a devoted friend of Elizabeth, she wrote after she had observed him giving a careless homily to a crowded church: "Do you remember a priest holds the honor of God on his lips? Do you not trouble yourself to spread his fire he wishes so much enkindled? If you will not study and prepare when young, what when you are old?"

As Dorothy Day noted in her column "On Pilgrimage," those years held much physical hardship for the little community. The sisters subsisted on carrot-coffee, salt port and buttermilk during one winter. For Christmas they had smoked sardines, and it was so cold a winter that snow by the barrelfull drifted through the crevices and into their rooms.

Mother Seton's health continued to decline; and, aware of her condition, she wrote Antonio Filicchi that death had been grinning at her for some time. To another friend she wrote, "St. Joseph's house is well established; it does not need even my nominal care."

On January 2, 1821, it was clear that Mother Seton was dying. To the sisters gathered around her she said, "Be children of the church! Be children of the church." At two o'clock in the morning of January 4 she died quietly. The little girl who had been born before the United States was a nation was reunited with the family and friends she had loved and lost. She left behind her fifty Sisters of Charity to continue her work.

On Sunday morning, September 14, 1975, the year before the bi-centennial celebration in the United States, Pope Paul VI declared Elizabeth Anne Bayley Seton a saint in the presence of hundreds of thousands of pilgrims, 20,000 of whom were American citizens. It was the canonization of an extraordinarily ordinary life, lived by a most unusual and spiritually gifted woman.

Theresa of Jesus Gerhardinger
1797–1879

SOMEONE has said that the lives of foundresses of religious orders are all the same; if you have read the biography of one you have read them all. In a superficial way this is true. Each saw a need in the church and the world; and, with the grace of God, her own intensity of purpose, prayer and sacrifice, and with a special charism which attracted others to her to work with her, she set about doing something specific about that need. Yet in reality, each is a special story. The accomplishments of each are particular to her and awesomely vast when one measures the brevity of time in which she accomplished what she set out to do.

Because I think my own foundress, Theresa of Jesus Gerhardinger, although she was a 19th century European woman, is a role model for us in the 20th-century, I have decided to include her in this book. She would have smiled indulgently and shaken her head in a gentle negation had anyone in her own day called her a genius; but, having spent five years editing her more than 5,000 letters (the phone had not been invented, so all her business and personal communication had to

131

be by mail), I have no hesitation in attaching that description to her.

Like all geniuses, she did not fit the mold. She was humane and charming, but also fiercely committed to her convictions—so much so that she was forced by her conscience to adhere to them, even when the weight of ecclesiastical disapproval seemed to be against her. Her beatification on November 17, 1985, put the stamp of approval upon her instincts; and the 7,500 School Sisters of Notre Dame in 34 countries around the world who are still working out her apostolate underscore the rightness of her vision.

Theresa was born on June 20, 1797, in the little city of Stadtamhof, across the Danube from Regensburg. Her father was a successful shipwright; his wife, Frances Huber, a young woman from nearby Abensberg. The young couple named their little girl Caroline, and since she was destined to be their only child we can be assured that they lavished love and care upon her. There is little in the records about her childhood, for Mother Theresa was not one to reminisce about herself.

At the age of six she was enrolled in the girls' school conducted by the cloistered Canonnesses of St. Augustine, more generally known as Notre Dame Sisters, founded by St. Peter Fourier. Caroline was a good student, and the sisters occasionally put the little girl on the "turn" and brought her into the enclosure where she was allowed to see how the sisters lived. Even if she admired them, and may have had childhood fantasies about joining them one day, she certainly never dreamed that when they were expelled she would revive the Order in a modified form. That she must have shown some extraordinary spirituality even as a child is evidenced by the fact that at a time when children were permitted to receive Holy Communion only when they reached adolescence, Caroline's was the unusual privilege of making her First Communion when she was only nine.

She was not quite twelve years old when the French and Bavarian armies under Napoleon repulsed the Austrians in 1809; and the defeated army began to retreat through Regensburg, across the bridge near Caroline's home. Napoleon bombarded the city; and flames soon swept over it, igniting a few homes in Stadtamhof as well with a light that illuminated her home. The family prayed not only for safety, but for the fleeing soldiers; and Caroline joined her father in the garret to view the conflagration. It was her introduction to war; but, given the tensions in Europe at the time, it was not to be her last.

A few months after the night of horror Caroline finished the elementary school course with honor. As a special treat her father took her with him to Vienna when he made a business trip there, a trip which was to be the first of a lifetime of long and tiresome journeys in the service of God.

On August 1, 1809 the Bavarian commissary ordered the suppression of the Order of Notre Dame; and the government seized the property of the sisters, allowing them a few weeks to obtain dispensations from their vows and make preparations for their future lives. On August 30, the nuns, wearing secular clothes, and carrying parcels with their few personal effects, left the convent school in which they had hoped to end their lives.

This would scarcely have seemed the moment for anyone to consider founding an order of religious women; but Bishop Michael Wittmann of Regensburg, a friend of the Gerhardinger family, watching the sisters dispersed by the government, had a dream of a new foundation with a mitigated Rule which would permit the sisters to live in smaller numbers. In this way they could accommodate children in small towns and villages who could not afford to travel to the larger cities, where the monastic rules obliged existing orders to live.

Saints may be visionaries, but they are also very practical. Bishop Wittmann asked the Gerhardingers if they would not like to have Caroline receive further education, since she had given indication of a quick mind and scholarly instincts, as well as a warm heart and concern for the poor children whose needy parents often received food and clothing from her own father and mother.

Caroline was interested; and she and two of her classmates, Anna Hotz and Anna Braun, were tutored by the bishop and one of his assistants, Rev. George Mauerer. When they were considered competent to teach, the bishop suggested they take charge of a small school for girls. It was a flattering suggestion. Although Caroline had some reservations about being restricted by the regularity of the classroom after her introduction to the wider world outside Stadtamhof with her father, after talking it over with her parents she agreed; although, with her lively temperament, she had no intention of devoting her life to the monotony of teaching.

Bishop Wittmann, who knew his young parishioner, wisely made no suggestion about the possibility of such a life-time commitment; but he encouraged the young women, and was delighted when, after a public examination, they received a certificate from the government entitling them to teach and another appointing them teachers in the city girls' school.

In the meantime he had confided his dream of a congregation to educate poor girls to his friend, Rev. Sebastian Job, chaplain to the Empress of Austria. Job, a scholar, was caught up in the plan and promised not only his moral support but also such financial aid as he could give.

While he and the bishop conferred, the change in Caroline which Bishop Wittmann had foreseen was occurring. As children came to them, illiterate and knowing almost nothing of God, she began to ponder what she could do to improve what she considered a frightening moral and intellectual need. When her father died in 1825 and her mother came to keep house for her and her companions, Caroline was overcome by a strange and compulsive urge to give herself to God and in so doing to give herself to the children whose poverty was a constant reproach to her.

When Caroline confided her misgivings to Bishop Wittmann he did not tell her he had anticipated them. He assured her that her inspiration was from God, and that perhaps she and her companions might live under an adaptation of the Rule of her former teachers, an adaptation Father Job was even then working on. The new provisional Rule by which the young women were to live allowed considerable flexibility; and both Father Job and the bishop did not want it submitted for ecclesiastical approval until it had been tested by living for several years to check its practicality, and after such changes in it as seemed feasible were made. The major difference between the new Rule and that of existing religious orders was that individual houses were to be neither autonomous nor diocesan, but were to achieve unity with diversity through a central Generalate which would provide formation, training, and support when this became necessary. It was a radical idea at that time, and was to cause Caroline great difficulties in the future.

In 1818 a Concordat between Bavaria and the Holy See permitted the reestablishment of convents for women whose members devoted themselves to teaching or the care of the sick. Caroline immediately applied for permission to begin religious life with her companions, and the plan was approved. She spent the summer holidays visiting convents in Hallein, in Austria, and the Carmelite convent at Gmunden, where she was so captivated by the life that she was almost tempted to believe her vocation was to contemplation, not to the active work of teaching.

But her sense of responsibility to the children she had known pulled her back; and she and two companions left Stadtamhof for Neunburg vorm Wald, Father Job's birthplace, where he had endowed a small motherhouse and school. All appeared to be going well, but that soon changed. Without warning the small community lost its strongest supports; both

Bl. Theresa of Jesus Gerhardinger

Bishop Wittmann and Father Job died before the little group of women had even taken vows. Caroline's mother lived with them; and her generosity kept them fed—and one suspects, clothed—but she was growing older, and obviously her endowment could not be taken for granted.

At night, when Caroline thought her companions were asleep, she would go quietly to the sacristy of the church to pray for God's guidance on this strange new path to which he was inviting them. In her journal we find a prayer which she said often during these night hours: "O Jesus, the greatest of all commitments lies before me. I should be poor in spirit, and poor in spirit I wish to be. But of myself I cannot achieve this. Therefore I pray, Lord, empty me of myself; give me yourself. Give me Jesus in the Holy Spirit."

Another prayer in the journal which indicates her state of mind before finalizing this momentous decision: "Enlighten me, strengthen me, so that I may understand and know my divine call, who I am, what I should be, and what I must do, as well as the means by which these ends may be accomplished."

We, who are faced with equally crucial decisions in this last quarter of the 20th century, might well make this prayer ours.

While Caroline was praying, the people of Neunburg, when they realized that Father Job's financial support of the center would be curtailed by his death, suddenly decided they did not need the sisters. Anyone but a saint would have given up, believing the evidence to be obvious: the dream was just that—a dream. Caroline and her companions did not. They checked on the fund that Father Job had promised them; and while it was not as large as they had been led to believe, it was sufficient to keep them in existence. The Empress of Austria, who had learned about the group from her confessor, became their benefactor; and also persuaded her brother, the King of Bavaria, not only to approve the new religious institute but also to contribute to its maintenance.

With the crisis of their survival temporarily settled, the group felt secure enough to commit themselves to God and Christian education by vow. Caroline, as founder, took her vows the day before her companions, who now numbered seven. She received the name Theresa of Jesus. Caroline's novitiate had lasted twenty years; she was now thirty-seven years old.

The school at Neunburg was so successful, the teachers so dedicated, the students so contented and happy, that the good news spread. Before long requests came to Mother Theresa from pastors who had heard of the successful venture for sisters to come to their parishes to teach their children. She might have been forced to refuse, were it not that young women also heard of the Sisters of Notre Dame, who were so obsessed by their love of God and the children of God, and came in numbers asking to join the little company.

There is something spring-like in the early years of any spiritual endeavor, a happiness that is quite unusual and never duplicated when the work becomes stable. At any rate, in the six years in which the convent at Neunburg was the main house of the order, sixty postulants received the veil, and there were sisters teaching in eight branch houses. Some of the young

Bl. Theresa of Jesus Gerhardinger

women did not stay, of course; for, then as now, some were not strong enough to withstand the corroding effect of daily living, and fatigue and monotony nibbled away at the original good intentions. But there were enough who did stay so that it was necessary that the motherhouse be moved to a larger center.

Archbishop von Reisach of Munich, who had heard of Mother Theresa's congregation and saw it as an answer to pressing needs in the church, invited her to Munich; and, after some negotiations, offered her the old convent of the Poor Clares in the center of the city. King Ludwig financed the remodeling; and one suspects he was a little surprised when Mother Theresa presented him with extensive plans for its renovation which included not only apartments for postulants, novices and professed sisters, but an educational institute where the young women might be trained for their religious and educational future and schools on all levels where they could do their supervised practice teaching. At any rate, he is quoted as saying of her, "This woman knows what she wants, and what she wants is well-thought out, indeed."

The next years were filled with inevitable problems. While incredibly mortified herself, she was insistent that the parishes to which she sent her sisters provide them with sufficient nourishing food and a warm convent with enough cords of wood to keep it so in the cold Bavarian winters.

Another demand which recurs increasingly in her letters seems to the contemporary reader to be a bit excessive: "The convent must be joined to the church, so that the sisters can attend Mass without going out on

139

the street." But when one reads the reason, in a letter of 1842, it reveals a realistic and concerned leader. She writes, "In branch houses where a private passageway to the church did not exist, the sisters have been forced to walk through crowded rows of men, some of whom mocked them, tripping them so that they fell, to the boisterous amusement of the bystanders. They have been pushed, had their veils torn off, and been the victims of snowballs viciously thrown at them as they went to church. In addition, they have been trapped in the arms of men, and had obscenities shouted in their ears." No wonder she demanded protection for her young women.

The work expanded. Mother Theresa could not fill all the requests for sisters. In 1841 she wrote, "More than forty school districts have asked for teachers, and we have had to put them off indefinitely." Her intention was to educate girls to become devout women, and "we are especially concerned about girls from the middle and lower classes, for whom other educational institutions are inaccessible." Before long the sisters were active in all areas of education and social service. They taught in grade schools, technical and vocational schools, and secondary schools; took care of infants and pre-school children in orphanages and kindergartens; and also became involved with rehabilitation centers. Their teacher-training institute in Munich was eventually open to college women as well as young sisters. They were busy, pressured years; and while for Mother Theresa the work was prayer, it was not the only prayer to which they were devoted.

The Eucharist had always been a center of her life;

and she and her first group of friends had made a midnight vigil every night, even before they became religious. One of the three volumes of selected letters is made up of her personal prayers, the sort of thing we call journal prayers today; and many of them have a modern touch, or, it might be better to say, a universal application. She received permission to have Perpetual Adoration in the Munich motherhouse, but, practical woman that she was, she warned Mother Caroline, her vicar in the United States, about introducing it here prematurely.

More than a century before the term "Global Village" became an "in" word, Mother Theresa was aware of its reality. As Phyllis McGinley points out, the saints take the Word of the Gospel literally; and Mother Theresa felt that "Go, teach all nations" was directed to her personally and to her sisters. She told the pope, "We go where we are invited;" and the invitations came from all over Europe. In Europe alone, at the time of her death in 1879, the congregation had schools in Germany, Austria, Hungary, Czechoslovakia, Poland, England and Italy; and of those she founded 112 are still in existence, still doing the work she inaugurated. She had been invited to send religious to Scotland and Brazil, but had to refuse for lack of personnel. But she did cross the Atlantic and installed the School Sisters of Notre Dame in Baltimore in 1847, just 14 years after she and her first sisters took their vows.

Each foundation produced its own problems, but probably the most difficult came from those in North America. To tell the story of the problems she encountered here would require a book. She had never before opened a convent school without visiting the place where it would be, without having consulted with the pastor, the families of the children, and the city fathers. But financially this procedure was out of the question when it came to making a trial trip across the Atlantic. Furthermore, she had no reason to doubt that the sisters were both needed and wanted on this vast continent, as German immigrants flooded the country. Bishop after bishop from America stopped at the Munich motherhouse, begging for teachers for the girls in their dioceses who were deprived of the benefits of Christian education. The Belgian Father General of the Redemptorists even went to the king to ask for School Sisters; and negotiations for the project began in April, 1847.

She appointed a superior to take her place during her absence, selected eight gifted young sisters to open the American mission and obtained letters from the king introducing them to the German consulate in New York. Confident of their welcome, they left Bremen for America and St. Mary's, Pennsylvania, where she had been told a convent and school awaited them. After what even the captain admitted was the stormiest voyage in his memory (and Mother Theresa was not a good sailor; she spent most of the time sick in her cabin), the ship arrived in New York on July 30, 1847.

She and her little band were welcomed by the German consul and his wife, and entertained by them during their short stay in New York. But what they learned from him made their future look bleak. St.

Bl. Theresa of Jesus Gerhardinger

Mary's, Pennsylvania, was under the jurisdiction of the Bishop of Pittsburgh, who had not been informed of their coming. They had no letters of recommendation; the bishops who had so casually invited them to come were thousands of miles away in the mid-west. The chancery office in Munich had forgotten to contact the Bishop of Pittsburgh to assure him that they were *bona fide* religious with many convents in Germany, although their new Rule was still in the experimental stage and not officially approved by Rome. The little colony of Germans in St. Mary's were destitute, and it was extremely doubtful that they could support even a small convent and school.

Mother Theresa, who had until now been known for her prudence and wisdom, appeared to the lay and churchmen she consulted as both impulsive and ill-advised. The little group was advised to turn back immediately to Europe. Mother, however, one of whose favorite sayings was, "All the works of God are accomplished by suffering," decided to obtain the permission of the bishop and to go on to St. Mary's to see things for herself. It was a difficult trip through deep forests and over rough roads; and before they reached St. Mary's the youngest of the sisters, Novice Edmunda, had succumbed to a fever and died within a day in a hotel in Harrisburg. They were obliged to have the funeral the next morning; and by afternoon the grieving sisters were again on their way, traveling through the wilderness through roads cut through the forest, a rough journey which lasted three days.

It was August 15 when they reached St. Mary's during an awesome thunderstorm. The colonists gave them the first enthusiastic welcome they had received since arriving in the United States. There were about 1400 settlers, whose 200 or so homes were rude log cabins and whose farms were a thing of the future, since the forest had to be cleared before plowing could be done. A rough building had been prepared for them, however; and Mother Theresa found young people, some of them 18 years old, who had not learned to read or write. She wrote to the king, "We will open school on September 20, free of charge of course, because the poor colonists have nothing with which to pay during our first years here."

The situation was serious; but Father Neumann, the Redemptorist provincial and later Bishop of Philadelphia, canonized in 1977, came to her rescue. It was obvious to Mother Theresa that St. Mary's could not be the center of their work in the United States. Through Father Neumann's influence she was offered two schools in Baltimore, but the convents Mother would have to provide for from her own resources. She wrote to the king, and the Mission Society responded with enough funds to keep the sisters until they should be self-supporting. Then, since it was obvious they would stay in America, Father Neumann invited Mother and 26-year-old Sister Caroline (whom she would appoint her vicar) to become acquainted with the vast country by traveling with him when he made his visitation of the Redemptorist houses.

They traveled for five weeks, covering 2500 miles by ox-cart, steamships, horses, and ferries, visiting Buffalo, Detroit, Chicago, New York and Philadelphia.

Bl. Theresa of Jesus Gerhardinger

Mother's letters home are descriptive, and indicate a rapid awareness of the difference between this country, with its pluralistic society, and the tight, centuries-old cultures of Europe which, although diversified, were historically united, even if lightly. There are amusing touches in her report, as when she notes that when they stopped at inns she always ordered the same thing; it was the only food she had learned to pronounce with confidence. She notes that she had been advised not to accept any school unless they were given $150 a year for each sister, since with less than that they could not exist. She is aware that "conditions here differ greatly from what people in Europe imagine them to be—a land with mountains full of gold where all one has to do is to settle in order to acquire extensive property and money."

In short, the years in the United States taught Mother Theresa much that would be valuable in the years ahead when her guidance would be from a distance, since she would never return. By now she was 51 years old, and the Rule was still not approved.

After much reflection and prayer she named 26-year-old Sister Caroline Friess her vicar for the American missions, realizing that it would take the energy and daring of a young woman to cope with the problems of this new country. During the years until her death the communication between the two was frequent, but Mother Theresa wisely refrained from giving specific directives to her vicar. She limited herself to advice, admitting that Caroline knew the situations better than she. Although this is not Mother

Caroline's story, it is interesting to note that one of the first things she did was to apply for naturalization papers in order to become an American citizen.

The rapid growth of the Congregation in the United States equalled that in Europe; and Mother Theresa's statement in a letter written from New York is an interesting one, "Deep in my heart is the realization that America will either give a great impetus to our Congregation, or will destroy it."

Upon her return to Munich her first concern was the approbation of the Rule which she and her councilors had finally refined after almost 20 years of lived experience. It was to develop into the most painful experience of her life, involving as it did a disagreement with an old and valued friend, the possible dissolution of the Congregation, and her own possible excommunication.

Mother Theresa's rule was built on the dream of Bishop Wittmann: that sisters might live in small towns, united in their training and bound together by their union under a Mother General who would know all the sisters and thus be able to assign them to their mission in accordance with their talents and temperaments.

Her friend, Archbishop von Reisach, who had invited her to Munich and helped her during the early years, felt differently. He was convinced that each bishop should have authority over the religious congregations in his diocese. He himself wrote a Rule to be submitted to Rome, which, while making this the focus of government, attempted to incorporate the re-

146

ligious and educational aspects of Mother Theresa's sisters, which he had observed to be successful both in his diocese and those others in which it had been introduced.

Mother Theresa saw at once that without a center for formation the sisters would soon be divided, as each bishop emphasized the aspect of their life which best conformed to his personal ideals. She tried to persuade the archbishop of the impracticality of his plan, destroying as it would the distinctive feature of the Congregation: its unity. His response was to declare that no novices would be permitted to take vows at the Munich motherhouse—a situation which would have destroyed the School Sisters of Notre Dame, since they would have had no new members.

In a dramatic confrontation with Mother Theresa and all the professed sisters in the motherhouse, the archbishop stated that from then on all the sisters were under his personal direction, adding, "I have the right to demand this obedience. I will punish with the most severe canonical censure everyone who opposes and disobeys these my commands." When Mother Theresa was asked to declare whether she would or would not accept the Rule which the bishop was composing, she replied, "I cannot."

Asked whether she, "a woman, a very weak woman, would want to lead the Congregation without ecclesiastical authority . . . so that you need no one above you?" she answered, "I submit to the church as heretofore." Pressed further she finally agreed to submit, "until the Holy See decides otherwise, according to our former observances." Each of the sisters signed the bishop's document with practically the same condition.

Mother was forbidden to leave the Munich motherhouse; and when she was urged by the sisters to ask to go to Rome to present her Rule to the Holy Father, she was refused under pain of excommunication. She wrote to the pontiff on June 6, 1852, and to Cardinal von Hohenlohe on August 31 asking his help. She sent Sister Margaret Cortona to Rome to present the Rule to the Congregation for Religious; she also persuaded Rev. Schels to go to Rome on her behalf. The matter dragged on for several years.

As one reads the long letters dealing with the approbation of the Rule, it is easy to forget that while this worry weighed heavily upon her, the works of the Congregation continued to need her guidance. A striking evidence of Mother Theresa's faith under difficulties is the fact that on days when she expresses her fear that the order is on the verge of dissolution, she will write two or three letters to pastors, accepting their invitation to open a school in their parish or village. Her letters during this time deal with the spiritual life of the sisters more than with the threatening cloud over them all.

Finally her faith was rewarded. On January 23, 1854, the Holy See approved the Rule and Constitution drawn up by Mother Theresa rather than that composed by the archbishop. That the archbishop, although mistaken in his belief that his way was best, was a man of God is evidenced by his bringing the document to Mother Theresa personally, asking as he put the new approved Rule in her hands, "Well, now, when can we have profession of the novices?"

The remaining years of her life were filled with the day-by-day concerns which the expanding Congregation brought. Her apostolate broadened to include not only the poor and middle classes, but any who needed what her sisters could give. She sent two sisters to educate the children of a noble family in their palace; accepted into the motherhouse school two black children who had been sold in a slave market in Cairo; and wrote a sharp letter to the Department of the Interior, which told her their admission was against the law. She said, "Our dear Lord had stepped in regarding the Negro children in question; he has taken one after the other home from this valley of tears by death. Our house physicians give as the cause of their death their leaving the tropics."

During the Austrian-Prussian war of 1866 and the Franco-Prussian War of 1870 she advised the sisters always to have their bags packed, ready to leave at a moment's notice, and to send boarding school pupils home during the hostilities. Although the sisters were not nurses, she allowed some of the schools to be closed and the sisters to help take care of the wounded, regardless of nationality.

The establishment of Bismarck's Kulturkampf threatened to phase out all Catholic schools; and her entire life-work must have seemed futile as school after school, including her teacher-training institute in the motherhouse, was closed by her government. But to the very end her trust overshadowed all adversities. In one of her last letters, written in 1878 when she was 81, she told the sisters, "We think of the encouraging words of the 90th Psalm, 'He has given his angels charge over you, to guard you in all your ways,' and Jesus' own words, 'I am with you all days.'"

During the last years of her life she had given more and more of the decisions of the Congregation to younger women; and she herself spent her time knitting, praying, advising, and listening, always listening with concern and interest. On May 9, 1879, she died, leaving behind her thousands who would remember her with love and a sense of loss.

On November 17, 1985, Pope John Paul II proclaimed to the thousands who had come from all over the world to hear his words that she was indeed a remarkable and holy woman; and the church, in his name, pronounced her blessed. At that moment a large picture of Mother Theresa was unrolled to hang on the wall of St. Peter's, to the applause of those gathered to do her honor. And I thought, as emotion swept over me, all this is for the woman who 133 years ago could not get ecclesiastical permission to travel to Rome to explain the Rule she and thousands of sisters who followed her had drawn up and lived for a lifetime in their quest for sanctity.

Edith Stein
1891–1942

A LITTLE girl who had been reading a child's book of saints remarked with conviction, "I'd rather be a martyr than a saint—it goes quicker." But those of us who remember the horror of the Holocaust, with its drawn-out fear, distrust of long-time friends and even on occasion of relatives, the slow trips in box cars in crowded, filthy conditions and the final terror of the inhumane execution, realize martyrdom is not always a speedy end. For Edith Stein—Jewish philosopher, Roman Catholic convert, teacher, author, and Carmelite nun—the end at Auschwitz was anything but quick.

On October 12, 1891, on the Jewish feast of the Atonement, Edith was born in Breslau, Silesia, now Poland, into a deeply devoted Jewish family of strong faith. Her father ran a successful timber business; but when he died two years after Edith's birth, the care of the business and of her seven children fell upon his wife, Augusta Courant Stein. She was a keen business-woman, and competitors admitted that she could estimate at a glance how many cords of wood might be obtained from a grove of trees.

Mary Hester Valentine

Edith's was a happy childhood, secure in the warm love of her mother and her six older siblings, to whom she was a charming plaything. Her unusual intelligence revealed itself at an early age. And her elder brother taught her the names of German poets and the titles of their works when she was four, and then delighted to see the amazement of family guests when she poured out her accumulated knowledge. In school she became accustomed to being first in any class, but was not unduly proud of the fact. On one occasion when she fell below that level she remarked to her mother, "Hilda got the best grades today; and I'm glad, because she doesn't have any mother."

She completed the course at Breslau at fifteen and received the highest marks; but she never received first place, unjust though it was, because, as her biographers conclude, the ugly face of anti-Semitism was already an issue in the town. Whether she was recognized or not, she had received an excellent education. She was fluent in French, English, Spanish, Latin, Greek, and, of course, Hebrew. In 1911 she passed the comprehensive examinations enabling her to enroll at the University of Breslau, where her areas of concentration were history, philosophy, and experimental psychology.

Although Edith's mother was pleased with her brilliant daughter's scholastic achievements, she was concerned because Edith no longer believed in God. Even though she continued to attend the synagogue with her mother, she did not participate in the service. Later she admitted that from the time she was thirteen until she was twenty-one she was an atheist, although she confessed that even in those years she had a constant yearning for the Absolute.

At the University in Breslau she was introduced to the writings of Edmund Husserl, especially his *Logical Investigations;* and her growing desire was to study under the master himself.

Husserl pointed young philosophers in a new direction: he went back to scholasticism, and, in opposition to the popular trends of the time, stressed the existence of objective truth and the knowable world in which we live.

Edith was told to contact Adolf Reinach, himself a distinguished scholar, and to persuade him to intercede with Husserl to take her on as a student at the University of Gottingen. Since her mother's cousin, Richard Courant, was a professor of mathematics at that university, her family raised no objections to her studying there.

At Gottingen, Husserl's teaching of existentialism and phenomenology opened her mind to the revelation of being. He taught Edith that truth is not the creation of one who perceives it, but it is an absolute in itself; and she was attracted to his theory and that of Heidegger. From 1913, when she was 21 and entered the university, Edith's whole being was straining for the truth. In addition to studying with Husserl she also had a class with Max Scheler, receiving from him the first light of the Gospels. Scheler was the son of a Jewish mother and non-Jewish father. While at school in Munich he had met a priest who influenced him with the beauty of Christian belief and baptized him.

Edith came under his influence shortly after his own

entrance to the church; and he introduced her to a world which, she said, "had remained completely unknown to me. It did not lead me towards the faith, but it opened up a realm of phenomena which I could no longer ignore."

She wrote her thesis on "Empathy," and wrote of that time, "People with whom I came into contact every day and whom I admired, lived in the world of faith; and I thought it at least deserved some investigation."

But in 1914 World War I interrupted her intellectual life. Husserl, who had been appointed to Freiburg, asked her to go with him to be his assistant. She had passed the examination at Freiburg *summa cum laude*, and she was delighted to accept Husserl's offer. It would be more expensive there, but as far as money was concerned she had no worries. She used to quote her mother's ancient Jewish pattern for getting along, "Save a little, spend a little, and give a little."

She was Husserl's assistant, taking the place earlier destined for Reinach, who was at the front; and the work with the master lasted for 18 months. Later Husserl wrote a testimonial for Edith, stating, "She gave me her valuable cooperation not only by putting my manuscripts into shape for publication, but also in my work as academic teacher. Dr. Stein has gained a far-reaching as well as profound philosophical knowledge, and is unquestionably well qualified for independent scholarly research and teaching."

In November, 1917, Reinach was killed in the war. Edith was asked to go through his papers to see which were ready for publication. In order to do so she came across much which indicated that he had been well on his way into the church, such as, "Doubtless one can point out historical and national limitations in every man, but not so in Jesus." When Edith returned to Freiburg she realized that she could no longer shelve the vital question, "What think you of Christ? Whose son is He?" She also realized that if she accepted Christ, her whole life—personal, familial and professional—would change. It was a personal struggle. She regarded her conversion as a matter between herself and God, and was always reluctant to speak about it.

She was already assured of a brilliant future. Her family was proud of her, her colleagues respected her, and her friends loved her. She was so unassuming that those less gifted were never hostile to the young intellectual. She realized that by embracing the faith much of this would be shaken, but that was not the problem. The eternal question was, "Is it Truth?"

Then he who said, "I am the Truth" stepped into her life and erased her doubts forever. She was visiting her dear friend Hedwig Conrad-Martius, herself a Catholic; and, not being able to sleep, Edith went to her hostess's library to choose something to read. The first book she picked up was the autobiography of St. Teresa; and she was so fascinated that she read all night, until in the early morning she had finished. It showed Edith what she had been searching for, the drawing of the soul to a center; and for Teresa the center was Christ with whom one is united in prayer and the Cross.

Later Edith was to write a curious passage relating to her personal experience, and one is left to wonder whether it describes that night in which all intellectual and spiritual darkness became light. She wrote, "There is a state of resting in God, of a complete relaxation of all mental effort, when one no longer makes any plans or decisions, where one no longer acts, but abandons all the future to the Divine Will. Perhaps I have been granted this state after an experience that was too much for my powers, so that it completely absorbed my spiritual vitality, and deprived me of all energy. Resting in God is something entirely new and peculiar. It is a feeling of being in safe keeping, of being delivered from all worry, responsibility, and need for action."

But for Edith conviction demanded action. She went to the parish church at Bergzabern, and, after having attended Mass, followed the priest into the presbytery and asked to be baptized. She was received into the church on New Year's day, 1922.

It was a day of complete peace for Edith, but one for which the price would be dear. United as she was to her mother with a special affection, she realized the knowledge that her favorite daughter had become a Catholic would be to her mother the complete betrayal. Painful though it was, Edith did not put off telling her mother what she had done; and when she did, that strong, capable woman, who had never allowed emotion to overcome her, silently bowed her head and wept.

Had she been free to follow where her heart beckoned, Edith would at once have followed her mentor, Teresa, into Carmel. But that suffering she could not put upon her mother yet.

Edith Stein

Her spiritual director, Canon Schwind, furthermore was against it, because in his view her outstanding philosophical gifts made it imperative she should stay in the world and contribute. He found a teaching position for her at a Dominican sisters' school at Speyer, and she taught there for eight years. She was a demanding teacher, but a gentle one. She treated her students as adults; and was honest, if sometimes scathing, in her evaluation of their work. To one young woman who had strung together a paper with citations from many authors Edith wrote, "The use of quotations proves that other people are clever." Sometimes the sisters noticed her praying late into the night in the convent chapel, and teaching the next day with enthusiasm as if she had enjoyed a good night's rest.

She was a lasting influence, not only on the young women whom she taught, but also upon the younger sisters; and she became something like an unofficial novice directress. She gave classes in Latin to both lay students and the sisters, and the prioress was so impressed by her that she invited her to give conferences to the novices on prayer and spirituality. She ate her meals with the students instead of in the privacy of her room; and the young people soon discovered that she almost never ate meat and was abstemious in other ways, frequently offering her sweet to a student with a well-known sweet tooth.

Outside Speyer scholars had not forgotten her; and Father Przywara, S.J., came to consult her on a translation of Newman's *Idea of a University*, upon which she was working. He reports his surprise on meeting her, for he had "never met anyone whose looks betrayed her race as little as those of Edith Stein; she might rather be compared to the statue of Uta in Naumburg cathedral." It was on this visit that he suggested she should translate St. Thomas's *Quaestiones disputatae, de Veritate*," of which there existed no German version; and he urged her not to go to manuals and interpreters but straight to St. Thomas.

Her name was known, and when her work on St. Thomas was passed around among scholars she was asked to lecture on Thomism. But it was her reputation as an authority on the position of women in modern society and in the church which really established her as a lecturer. She had been a feminist in her youth, and found talking to women very congenial. One of the most important of these lectures was to the Congress of the German Association of Catholic Graduates at Salzburg in 1930, and it was acclaimed as the high point of the Congress.

It became obvious to her as well as to her advisors that the convent at Speyer was no longer the place where God wanted her. She resigned from her post there and applied for a teaching position at the University of Freiburg, but was unsuccessful. The Educational Institute at Munster accepted her as lecturer in 1932, and from there she continued her work as lecturer on the task of women in today's world. In September, 1932, she went to the Thomist conference which was centering on Phenomenology and Thomism at Juvisy. There the scholars were particularly impressed by her clarity of thought and the ease with which she answered questions in either French or German.

Edith Stein

Her thoughts on women's work in the world were far ahead of her time. She opposed those who felt women's place was in the kitchen, at church, and exclusively with the children; and stated that that attitude was prejudiced and that those who held it were simply unwilling to examine the facts. She felt strongly that "if need be, every normal and healthy woman can fill a post; there is none that could not be filled by a woman." She was especially emphatic in urging the need for women's influence in industry and factories, or in any work where the machine tends to make work dehumanizing.

When discussing the position of women in the church she stressed Christ's attitude, pointing out that he made no distinction between men and women. Her statements were so widely discussed that she could even seriously raise the question of the priesthood of women, saying, "Dogmatically it seems to me that nothing could prevent the church from introducing such an unheard-of novelty. Whether it could be recommended from a patently practical point of view would admit of many pros and cons."

Edith Stein's forceful presentation drew audiences to her. It was what she did not say as well as what she did and her overpowering personality, which convinced. One teacher wrote, "I expected to hear an imposing, self-confident female Jewish intellectual . . . and a fascinating speech, of course. But instead of a personality all set to captivate you with her method of presentation and intellectual brilliance, there appeared a small, delicate, surprisingly unpretentious woman, simply and tastefully dressed, who clearly had no intention of overwhelming you by her demeanor and her dazzling wit. Dispensing with psychological and anthropological findings, she transferred the question of woman's vocation from its religious context to one that presented men and women in their mutual complementarity and their individual responsibility before God."

Edith enjoyed these opportunities, but the convert yearned to be free for that aspect of Christian life which is love, not learning. Wherever she was, people saw that quality in her; and many came to her for help: the poor, the sick, especially those who sought advice in spiritual matters. She gave away whatever she could, not only clothes but books and whatever her modest salary left her for almsgiving. She never forgot a birthday, or, after she became a Catholic, a feast day of a friend. Every summer she went home to Breslau to do what she could to ease the pain her conversion had caused her mother.

Her greatest joy was in the Benedictine abbey of Beuron, where she went many times after her first visit in Holy Week, 1928. She followed the Order of the monastery and even exceeded it on occasion, as when she spent the entire Good Friday in the abbey church. When some commented on it she answered that this was the practice of devout Jews on the Day of Atonement; she had seen her mother do it many times. Certainly she felt that as a Catholic she could share with Christ the day he redeemed the world.

Finally, as anti-Semitism became more public in Germany, and her presence in a Catholic university and on a lecture platform became more an embarrassment than a help, she decided that now she was free to fulfill her desire to become a Carmelite.

On January 30, 1933, when Hitler took over full powers in Germany and immediately began to enact anti-Jewish laws, Edith conceived the plan of going to Rome and in private audience asking the Holy Father for an encyclical on the Jewish question. She was told she could not hope for a private audience, so she contented herself with writing a letter to the pope. Almost five years later she told her prioress in the Cologne Carmel, "I know my letter was delivered to the Holy Father; I received his blessing for myself and my family some time afterwards. But nothing else happened."

She planned to wind up her affairs by July 15 so that she could celebrate the feast of Our Lady of Mount Carmel, July 16, at Cologne. She stayed as a guest for about a month and then went home to Breslau for the last heart-breaking farewell to her mother.

When Edith told the aging woman of her intention old Frau Stein broke down completely, and the Church and the Synagogue confronted each other. Her mother asked, "Can one not also be devout in the Jewish way?"

"Certainly, if one has not come to know anything else," answered Edith.

And then, the desperate, infinitely pathetic reply of her mother, "Why did you come to know it? I won't say anything against Him. He may have been a very good man. But why did He make Himself God?" Mrs. Stein's suffering was not only that she was losing her daughter, but, good Jew that she was, it seemed that the daughter was turning her back on Yahweh.

Edith herself reports that that evening, when all visitors had left, her mother's self-control gave way. She covered her face with her hands and began to weep. "I stood behind her chair and placed her silver white head against my breast. So we remained a long time, until she let herself be persuaded to go to bed. . . . I do not think either of us had any rest that night."

On her way home she had broken her journey to attend a Holy Hour. She described the experience: "I spoke to Our Lord and told him that I knew it was his cross that was being laid on the Jewish people. Most of them did not know that, but those who did ought to embrace it willingly in the name of all. This I desired to do. He should only show me the way." When her devotions were finished she had an interior certainty that her prayer had been answered. Her going to Carmel was the first step, certainly, and the farewell to her mother the Agony that preceded it.

She was received as a novice at the Carmel in Cologne and professed her vows five years later. She was 42 years old; her juniors by 20 years were more effective in their duties than she. Most of the sisters did not know the illustrious woman who had accomplished so much for the church, and this as well as her awkwardness in this new life must have been difficult for her. But she adapted herself to the customs of the house, and accepted her limitations with humor. At her clothing she so impressed Gertrud von le Fort by her air of complete serenity that she kept a photo of her on her desk during the writing of her book, *The Eternal Woman.*

Edith, now Sister Teresa Benedicta of the Cross, suffered interiorly as Hitler's anti-Semitism swept the country; and she realized that her family could not understand her leaving them just when Jews were beginning to suffer bitter persecution. It seemed to them, especially to her mother, the final betrayal.

The Father Provincial of the Carmelites asked Sister Benedicta to take up intellectual work again, and she was assigned writing as her community apostolate. Her most beautiful works date from this time: *The Mystery of Christmas, Eternal and Infinite Being, The Science of the Cross,* and *Hymns to the Church.* She also took up an apostolate of letter writing: to former students, to friends and family who were suffering. Running through them was a central theme: "Do everything you can to give joy to others; let God guide you without resistance; fill up the emptiness of your heart with love of God and neighbor."

Edith's brother, her sister Erna, and children left Germany before the persecutions got under way. On November 9 the pogroms broke out and the Cologne synagogue was burned. Edith wrote, "The shadow of the Cross has fallen over my people." It had also fallen over her. With much reluctance the Cologne Carmel decided Edith would be safer in Holland; and, reluctant though they were to see her leave, arrangements were made and she left for the Carmel in Echt. Initially it was difficult for both the sisters and Edith, for she was a complete stranger. Her sister Rosa, who had joined the church after their mother's death, came to Holland with Edith and served as an extern. There was uneasiness in the house, for the sisters learned from Rosa of the war and persecutions; and some felt that both she and Edith would attract unfavorable attention to the convent.

But Sister Benedicta soon became invaluable. The Carmelite superiors sent word that in all the Dutch convents Dutch should be spoken in chapter and at recreation. The older German sisters had never bothered to learn the language; and when Sister Benedicta, who learned it quickly, helped those who were slower in grasping its intricacies, she became indispensable. They began to appreciate Rosa as well, for she was as practical in domestic affairs as her sister was not; and her detachment and good humor helped lift the pressure of the impending occupation.

Sister Benedicta wrote her friends, "We leave everything trustfully to Providence and quietly go about our duties."

But by 1941 Holland was in the grip of the German army; raids on England were made from the Dutch coast almost every night. At the end of the year it was decided that it would be safer for both Rosa and Sister Benedicta to move again, this time to the Swiss Carmel at Le Paquier. The Carmel was small, and word came to Echt that there would be room for Sister Benedicta but that they would have to make other arrangements for Rosa. By the time a place was eventually found for her in another convent of 3rd Order Carmelites it was too late: the Gestapo had ordered both the "Stein women" to appear at Nazi headquarters in Maastricht.

Edith Stein

When they entered the office, Sister Benedicta greeted the officers with "Praised be Jesus Christ," instead of "Heil Hitler." It was an imprudent gesture, though the outcome would probably have been no different had she given the Nazi salute; and it is refreshing to know she was a woman ready to make such a fearless profession of faith to the dreaded Gestapo. They were shouted at because their identity cards did not have the red "J" marking them as Jews and because they had not added "Sarah" to their names, which was now the law for all of Jewish origin. They were then issued the yellow Star of David and ordered to wear it at all times, and to appear again for questioning, this time in Amsterdam. The interviews became more frequent. Sister Benedicta's peace remained unshaken, although she was very concerned for Rosa, whose faith was no less than hers but upon whom the strain was beginning to tell. A business man, a friend of the sisters, tells how on one occasion when he waited for a train with the two he was so impressed by Sister Benedicta's calm before the coming ordeal that he said, "Today I have spoken to a saint."

The cat and mouse game came to an abrupt end when a general order was issued for mass deportation of Dutch Jews.

We have read it all before; Anne Frank's diary gives the details of the hunted desperately seeking for places to hide from the hunters. When the storm broke Sister Benedicta did not hide; she had anticipated this for a long time. A friend who told her how happy she was to see her safely behind the grille of the Carmel was answered with, "Don't believe it. They will come after me even here. In any event, I don't count on being spared."

She received the sad news on July 28 that one of her brothers and his family had been taken to the concentration camp of Theresienstadt; and she knew that for her, too, the end was near. She had composed her final testament and was ready. The document concludes with, "I joyfully accept in advance the death God has appointed for me in perfect submission to his most holy will. May the Lord accept my life and death for the honor and glory of his name, for the needs of his holy church . . . for the Jewish people, that the Lord may be received by his own, and his kingdom come in glory, for the deliverance of Germany and peace throughout the world, and finally, for all my relatives living and dead, all whom God has given me; may none of them be lost."

Throughout Holland there was a growing resistance to the deportations. Catholic and Protestant church leaders agreed to send a joint telegram to the German authorities protesting the action. Their telegram reads in part, "The undersigned Dutch churches, profoundly disturbed by the measures already taken against the Jews of the Netherlands, by which they have become excluded from the ordinary life of the nation, have now learned with horror of the proposed action which would evacuate men, women, children and entire families into German territory. . . . These measures are contrary to the deepest convictions of the Dutch people and God's demands of justice and mercy, and compel us to urgently petition you not to have this directive carried out. In the case of Christians of Jewish descent we are moved by a further consideration: namely, such measures would sever them from participation in the life of the church."

The exception was honored for a brief time, but the inhuman treatment of the other Jews so weighed on the Archbishop of Utrecht that, after wrestling with his conscience, he wrote a pastoral letter protesting the unjust actions against Dutch citizens.

On August 2, as reprisal for the pastoral, all non-Aryan Catholics were arrested throughout Holland. In the Carmel at Echt at five in the evening, the prioress was called to the parlor, where two storm troopers called for Sister Benedicta. The prioress, thinking it had to do with her emigration to Switzerland, called for Sister Benedicta. She realized the real purpose of the visit when Sister Benedicta was ordered to be ready to leave the convent within five minutes. When she insisted that it was not possible she was given ten minutes. Assisted by several other nuns she packed a rug, a mug, a spoon, and food sufficient for three days. When she left the enclosure she found her sister, Rosa, who was also being deported, kneeling to receive the blessing of the prioress.

From the local police department they were taken in two police vans which carried 13-17 people to Amersfoort. They arrived at three in the morning; and the soldiers there, weary no doubt from having had to wait up for their prisoners, beat them with rifle butts and drove them into dormitories without any food.

Three days later the Carmelites sent two men from Echt with warm clothes and medicine to the concentration camp, which, fortunately, was guarded by

Dutch police who allowed the sisters to meet the messengers and to receive the gifts.

During the month attempts to find out what happened to Sister Benedicta met with little success. In March, 1947, Dr. Lenig, who had been interned at Amersfoort at the same time and was the only person released from custody, gave the following report:

"On August 7, 1942, Valentine Fouquet, then stationmaster in Schifferstadt, was standing on the platform when a train from Saarbrucken pulled in with a sealed compartment carrying prisoners. A woman in dark clothing hailed him and asked whether he knew the family of Dean Schwind. When he said he did the woman asked him to give Edith Stein's greetings to the dean and his family, and to inform them she was on her way east."

Another article in 1982 by Johannes Wieners fills in a bit more of the lost days. Wieners was with the Cologne postal service. On August 7, 1942, while waiting in the railroad yard in Breslau, he saw a freight train on the track alongside him. "When the guard opened one of the sliding doors we could see people all penned up, listlessly squatting on the floor. There was a horrible stench. A woman dressed like a nun appeared at the door. . . . She said to me, 'It's terrible. We don't even have containers to relieve ourselves.' After that she looked into the distance at Breslau, and said, 'This is my home; I'll never see it again.' She paused for a moment, then said, 'We are going to our death.' . . . When I got back from internment in 1948 I read about Edith Stein in a magazine. The minute I saw her picture I knew it was the sister I saw August 7,

Edith Stein

1942. The day the article gave for her death was August 9."

A Dutch official who had been at Amersfoort spoke of her resignation and courage. "The one sister who impressed me, whose warm, glowing smile has never been erased from my memory, despite the disgusting incidents I was forced to witness, is the one I think the Vatican may one day canonize. From the moment I met her I knew there is some one truly great. For the time she lived in that hell hole, walking, talking and praying . . . like a saint. When I asked if there were anything I could do she answered, 'Why should baptism be allowed to become an advantage here?'"

On August 6 she managed to get a few lines through to the prioress, telling of the departure of the first convoy for Silesia or Czechoslovakia. Another undated message contained simply, "I am quite content now. One can only learn the Science of the Cross if one truly suffers under the weight of the Cross."

She made a striking impression among her companions in the camp by her calm and composure. She walked about among the women, comforting, helping, soothing. Many mothers were almost demented, and had for days not looked after their children. Sister Benedicta took care of the little ones, washed them, combed their hair, and saw to it that they got care and attention.

At Schifferstadt on August 7 one of her former pupils stood on the station platform. She heard herself called by her maiden name, and, looking around, recognized Edith Stein at the window of a train, calling to her, "Give my love to the sisters. I am traveling east." In

August also, Sister Adelgundis Jaegerschmid received a scrap of paper with a message scribbled in pencil, "Greetings from my journey to Poland. Sister Benedicta."

After that there was no more. On August 9, 1942, Sister Benedicta of the Cross and her sister, Rose, disappeared into the gas chamber at Auschwitz.

In 1962 Cardinal Frings of Cologne introduced her cause, and the results were submitted to Rome in 1972. Last week I received a letter from a friend in Rome who said, "It is very probable that Edith Stein will be beatified next year during the trip of the Holy Father to Germany. According to the program, which is not yet finalized, the beatification will take place in Cologne." How appropriate that she should be recognized in the city where she became a Carmelite and took vows. She is a patron of Jews, of non-believers, of intellectuals, of women, of everyone seeking the truth.

Dorothy Day
1897–1980

A T the end of her long and busy life Dorothy Day
once overheard someone remark that she was a
saint; she turned immediately and said sharply, "Oh,
no, don't write me off that easily." To her, being called
a saint meant being put on a pedestal to be admired
and ignored. She did not mind being labeled Moscow
Mary, atheistic Communist, Nigger lover; but prema-
ture canonization had no place in her active life. A
complex personality, her responses to people and the
complex society in which she lived were original, radical, and always a little challenging, not only to others,
but especially to herself. Now that she can no longer
object, people in increasing numbers are beginning to
call her "saint." Alive, she was certainly one for those
living in the Bowery.

The third in a family of five, Dorothy was born at
Bath Beach, Brooklyn on November 8, 1897 to John
Day, a horse-racing journalist, and Grace Satterlee
Day. The roots of both parents were deep in America,
and had she so wished Dorothy might have been a
member of both the Daughters of the American Revolution and the United Daughters of the Confederacy;

but from childhood her interests were strongly aimed at the here and now.

In 1904 the family moved to Oakland, California, only to move to Chicago after the San Francisco fire destroyed the newspaper for which John Day was writing. Dorothy always thought of her childhood as a happy one. While their fortunes fluctuated, and they lived in four different residences, one at least in a decidedly impoverished neighborhood, her mother's ability to make a pleasant home anywhere probably contributed to Dorothy's good memories of what might otherwise have been a bleak time.

Her parents were not religious, although her father always kept his Bible and her mother's Episcopalian background led to an enterprising pastor's locating the family. For a short time Dorothy and her brothers and sisters attended church with some regularity if not with enthusiasm. In adolescence she decided it was all artificial, and after reading Jack London and Upton Sinclair she gave up all religious affiliation.

Her years at Waller High School were uneventful. She does not refer to them in any of her writings, and apparently she formed no close friendships there. Her graduation in 1914 was apparently a routine affair. An examination sponsored by the *Examiner* won her a scholarship to the University of Illinois in Urbana, and at sixteen Dorothy Day was on her own.

It was an exciting experience to be independent, but with insufficient funds to maintain her status with dignity she was forced to supplement the scholarship by working. And work she did, doing a huge family laundry which rubbed her knuckles raw but gave her board and room and baby sitting for a faculty member's family until the solicitations of the father forced her to find another place to live. A small, unheated room in an attic was hers for a while; and although she suffered from the cold, she reveled in the luxury of privacy, which allowed her to read, read, read.

The scholastic aspect of the university she found boring. She was unfortunate in her professors, although her acknowledged competence and flair for writing encouraged her to apply for a position on the *Scribblers*. Her second year at Urbana was happier. She had met a friend, Rayna Simons, whose flaming hair, remarkably glowing eyes, warm, outgoing disposition and brilliant mind attracted Dorothy. They were both concerned about the social order, although Rayna, the Jewish daughter of a successful broker and one time vice-President of the Chicago Board of Trade, did not have any personal experience of poverty. Rayna brought Dorothy into the circle of her friends: Samson Raphaelson, her fiance; students who put out the *Daily Illini* and had "advanced ideas;" and young instructors who introduced them to exciting reading and spent long nights discussing revolutionary ideas and their practical application. Rayna insisted that Dorothy share her room in a boarding house for Jewish girls. Dorothy commented in later years that it was her first experience of anti-Semitism, for surely Rayna with her money, her background, her brains would have been invited to join a sorority were she not Jewish.

It was an entirely different year for Dorothy. She

and Rayna shared everything: clothes, friends, ideas, enthusiasm, and the long, long talks of youth. At the end of the year, however, Dorothy felt she had had enough of university life, even though it meant leaving Rayna. When Rayna died in 1928 in Russia, where she had gone to live, Dorothy grieved for her friend; but by then she had traveled from the University of Illinois.

Her family moved back to New York, and Dorothy went with them but did not live with them. She got a job writing for the *Call*, a socialist paper with limited money and an even more limited reading public. She had persuaded her editor, Chester Wright, to take her on, even though the paper could not afford another employee. She suggested she would live on $5 a week for a month, and write a report of each day's difficulties for the paper. The articles did not last out the month: it is hard to maintain daily interest in shopping for a quarter's worth of food. But Dorothy stayed on, contributing to a paper she later described as having no real socialist philosophy. They supported the AF of L, the Amalgamated Clothing Workers, the "Wobblies," and a vaguely anarchistic point of view. Dorothy herself was not a joiner, but she did go to lectures by Mike Gold, Elizabeth Flynn, Emma Goldman, and Ethel Byrne, Margaret Sanger's sister, whose birth control clinic was raided and who, when arrested, went on a hunger strike. All made good stories for the young reporter, and she might have really made a scoop had the interview she had with Trotsky been printed. As it was, Trotsky's socialism was diametrically opposed to the American brand. The editor of the *Call* rejected

Trotsky, and Dorothy's story went into the waste basket. The *Call* itself collapsed shortly afterwards when the postal department sent word its mailing permit was being revoked.

But by then Dorothy was well known, and had become involved with the Columbia University students' demonstrations against what appeared to be America's coming involvement in World War I. This was the first time, but not the last, that she would be engaged in opposition to the idiocy of war.

Charles Wood, drama critic for the *Masses*, introduced her to Floyd Dell, who invited her to be his assistant editor at ten dollars a week. Max Eastman was the actual editor; and it was he who had brought the magazine to its position as the voice of the new generation, emancipated from the past with its outdated morals and narrow-minded attitudes and judgments. The magazine was definitely left, and attracted writers with similar leanings. The aspect which fascinated Dorothy was its fearless, laughing tone. She had a challenging, and, she felt, an important job influencing young America in its job of changing the stodgy thinking of its elders.

She had a circle of East Side friends and felt at home in Greenwich Village, which was just emerging as a gathering place for the young artists of the decade. On November 9, 1917 in a Village restaurant Dorothy met Peggy Baird, who was on her way to join a woman suffragist movement in Washington which intended to picket the White House. Dorothy was invited to join them, and while she had no personal commitment to the cause it sounded like an exciting confrontation against "the system." At the party headquarters Dorothy learned that when, not if, they were jailed the women should go on a hunger strike, objecting to American women's being treated as criminals for speaking out for their rights. They were arrested, as anticipated, sentenced to a month's imprisonment, and taken to the workhouse, Occoquan Prison, which had a deservedly grim reputation. Dorothy fought incarceration physically, biting and kicking the jailer. While the dedicated suffragists were exhilarated by their situation, Dorothy felt nothing but disgust—for the cold, the brutality of the jailers, the gnawing hunger, the shouts of the other prisoners, and the nightmares which shattered her sleep every night. She asked for and received a Bible, reading it, she said, for its literary value; but she admitted it brought her peace, and she had "a sense of coming back to something of my childhood that I had lost." Six days after their imprisonment the group was transferred to the prison hospital; and Peggy persuaded Dorothy to break her fast, since the White House had changed their status from criminals to political prisoners, and the women felt they had won their cause.

The experience ended with Dorothy's making a firm decision: she would never, never again go to jail for a cause for which she was not willing to suffer. She would be jailed many times with Catholic Worker companions, but always having known it might be the outcome of a demonstration, always for a cause her whole being believed in, and always to make a statement she felt badly needed to be made to an indifferent world.

Dorothy Day

She returned to Greenwich Village and her friends; but it was a period of her life she was reluctant to discuss, because, as she said, she did not want her example during these years to be publicized so as to beguile young people. However, as William Miller points out, her deportment during the Village period was almost exemplary. She enjoyed the good fellowship of the writers who were convinced they were going to bring about a new world. Floyd Dell and Max Eastman were still there, as was Malcolm Cowley, Mike Gold, and Eugene O'Neill, whose moving recitation from memory of Francis Thompson's "Hound of Heaven" she remembered long after the playwright was dead. Eugene was dependent on Dorothy, and on a number of occasions she was one of the friends who helped the inebriated artist to bed. Some have thought that Josie Hogan in O'Neill's "Moon for the Misbegotten" was based upon Dorothy. However, the truth probably is that, like all his fictional characters, Josie is a combination of many of O'Neill's friends; and Dorothy may be only one of them.

Physically there is no resemblance. By now Dorothy Day was a young adult, 21 years old, tall, beautifully and strongly built, with unusual slanting eyes and clean sharp bones. She was never pretty; but she was always a striking personality in the full meaning of that term, even in later years when she was wearing clothes from the donations given to the Catholic Worker house. Hers was a presence novelists like to describe as, "When she came into the room people turned to look."

Dorothy herself said of her relationship with

O'Neill, "He gave me an intensification of the religious sense that was in me. And since he brought me such a consciousness of God . . . I owe him my prayers."

During these Greenwich Village years she puzzled her friends by slipping into Catholic churches and sitting in the back pews for long periods of time. Some have suggested it was because the churches were warm, but there were other possibilities—such as the public library—and Dorothy chose the church. Something was changing her, something very personal about which she could not talk with any of her friends.

In 1918 she and Della decided to take up nurses' training at King's County Hospital, Brooklyn. She remained a pacifist; but she did not think of nursing the suffering, especially the suffering poor, as a contribution to the war effort. It was a difficult period which demanded all her physical resources. They worked a 12-hour day, making beds, bathing the sick, helping feed the elderly and soothing the thousands who were dying of the worst influenza epidemic the world had ever experienced. But it was during this period that she had her first passionate love affair.

From her university days discussions about sex had rolled around her, and with the Greenwich Village crowd it was a topic about which one could philosophize endlessly. Dorothy had always stayed aloof from these discussions; she felt with her whole being that sex could only have meaning when it was accompanied by a passionate love between both persons. Now that passion had overwhelmed her.

Lionel Moise, an orderly in the hospital, whose rugged features Dorothy thought resembled those of

Amenemhat III, was a swashbuckling man of the world; he liked women, but was not disposed to be tied to any one of them. Dorothy persisted, and left the hospital so that she might be free when his irregular hours permitted their being together. The affair was a short-lived one, and its conclusion left Dorothy shattered. She had become pregnant, and delighted at the prospect of a child, she told Moise. He, however, was not about to be tied down by a family, and insisted that if she wanted to remain with him, she would have to agree to an abortion. It was a no-contest with Dorothy, and she submitted to the sordid business against her will. The doctor and his assistant left the building, and Dorothy waited for Moise to pick her up as he had promised. After hours of sitting in the empty waiting room, she realized he was not coming and made her way back to the apartment they shared to find a check and a farewell letter.

She was devastated and on the rebound in 1920 married Barkeley Tobey, a promoter who sold ideas with ease but never seemed to be able to bring any to conclusion. During the year they were together he took Dorothy to Europe: to London, Paris and Italy; and while she reveled in her introduction to a different culture, they both acknowledged that the marriage had been a mistake. She left Barkeley, although, since he later married eight more times, it may have been he who left Dorothy.

In any case, she decided to return to Chicago. She wrote her semi-autobiographical novel, *The Eleventh Virgin*, and found various short-term jobs as a cashier for Montgomery Ward and even as a courtroom reporter. She was imprisoned briefly on the absurd charge of being a prostitute when she and a sick friend took the only available lodgings they could find in a building which the police raided because they had seen the two women going into it—a men's home owned by the I.W.Ws.

After Della joined her in Chicago the two decided to go to New Orleans. Dorothy had no difficulty getting a job as a reporter on the New Orleans *Item,* and was assigned to do a series of articles on the "taxi dancers" —a series so successful that the Women's Club and Business Association of the city shut down the dance halls. While she lived in New Orleans she began attending services at the cathedral, going to Benediction, reading a prayer book to understand what was happening, and saying a rosary which a Russian Jewish friend had given her as a Christmas gift.

When *The Eleventh Virgin* sold and she received $2500, she returned to New York and a kind of homecoming. Some of the old friends had left, but the Cowleys welcomed her back; and it was not long before she again knew everyone who was anyone in the Village: Caroline Gordon, Allen Tate, Hart Crane, Kenneth Burke, John Dos Passos—and a young friend of Thomas Wolfe, Forster Batterham, with whom she contracted a common-law marriage. He was English, an anarchist, and a marine biologist who preferred to be alone in a boat fishing rather than participating in the endless arguments that went on in the Village community.

With the money from her novel Dorothy bought an old wooden beach house on the west end of Staten

Island, and there she and Forster lived for four years, from 1925-1929.

For Dorothy it was an idyllic time; she found nature healing. She did not mind Forster's absences, and even became interested in his collection of marine life. Forster, however, resented what he perceived as her developing interest in religion; and he definitely did not want a family, although Dorothy, with the burden of the death of her baby by abortion weighing upon her continually, desperately wanted another child. She also resolved that if she had a baby, she would have it baptized: she would not impose upon it the desert of the heart which had been her experience. When she discovered that she was pregnant she was ecstatic; and while Forster was less so, he was not Moise: he did not leave her, although he withdrew into solitude more and more, returning after a day on the water only to crawl into bed. For Dorothy it was enough to have the comfort of his body and the growing realization of the child within her.

When the baby was born in March at the end of a harsh winter, spring was both outside and in Dorothy's heart. She says, "My joy was so great that I sat up in bed in the hospital and wrote an article for the new *Masses* about my child, wanting to share my joy with the world. The article appealed to my Marxist friends so that the account was reprinted all over the world in workers' papers."

Her resolution to have the baby baptized never faltered, and back at Staten Island she encountered a nun and asked her how she should go about the baptism. Sister Aloysia was very matter-of-fact about the whole thing, and explained that the church would have to have assurance that the baby would be brought up a Catholic. Dorothy then acknowledged that she, too, would like to join the church; and the long odyssey was over. There were instructions from the old Baltimore catechism and difficulties with her husband, who felt that were she to give herself unreservedly to God there would be little room in her heart for him. Finally, Tamar was baptized in July; and Forster even provided a little party with garden vegetables and lobster.

But the next few months were periods of intermittent tension, especially when Dorothy urged him to consent to officially marry her and Forster would have none of it. As Miller says of him, "He was an anarchist and an atheist, but he did not intend to be a liar or a hypocrite." Her brother John was living with them at the time; and he, too, was confused by this new absorption of his sister in God. The whole situation was impossible, and it was inevitable that it would end. In December Dorothy told Forster their life together was over.

The next day she took Tamar to the city, and on December 28 presented herself to the priest at Tottenville. Everything about that day was grey: the weather, and the emptiness in Dorothy's heart. She experienced none of the new convert's joy and peace, but she had made a decision and there was no turning back. The next day she made her first Communion, and although she did not yet know what direction her life would take she knew it would never be the same.

Now 30 years old, she was alone again, and not only independent, but with a child to support. Dorothy found a flat on the West Side for $10 a month. She synopsized novels for Metro-Goldwyn-Mayer, and was invited to Hollywood by Pathe to write dialogue; but she returned to New York thoroughly disillusioned about life in the movie capitol. She, Tamar, and her brother John spent two summers at the beach house, the second of which she spent cooking for the few Marist priests and brothers who lived a mile away.

About this time she met George Shuster, editor for *Commonweal*, who gave her stories and even sent her to Mexico to report on the new governmental policy toward religion. She lived with the poor; and was fascinated, not by the political aspects, but by the human interest elements she saw all about her. She met Diego Rivera, wrote a brief report of the meeting, and sent back stories of the incredibly strong place the Catholic Church had in the lives of the people and of the beautiful and distinctly native celebration of Holy Week, with its exuberance of flowers and singing—this in spite of government proscription.

Back in New York in 1931 she bought a car, and she and Tamar enjoyed driving from New York to the beach house on Staten Island. It was a period of contentment and peace; and, still employed by Shuster, she continued to write: of the Hunger March on Washington, of the protests of small farmers for *America*, and a number of stories on the red-scare mentality of the country at the time—a mentality which distressed her, since she saw in it the seed of prejudice which would harm the innocent, the underpaid workers, and the destitute.

She wrote, "How strange it is that the Catholics who

begin to realize their brotherhood and take themselves to the poor and all races are accused of being Communists. When the demonstration was over I went to the national shrine at the Catholic University on the feast of the Immaculate Conception. There I offered up a special prayer, a prayer which came with tears and anguish, that some way would be open for me to use what talents I possessed for my fellow workers and for the poor." It was a prayer that was almost immediately answered. When she reached home she found a short, broad-shouldered workingman with a high, broad head covered with graying hair, a weather-beaten face, warm gray eyes, and a wide, pleasant mouth talking to her brother and his wife and Tamar. It was Peter Maurin, and Dorothy's life would never be the same.

He had heard about Dorothy from George Shuster, and decided, sight unseen, that with her good will and open mind and his dream of a personalist society they might join forces for the renewal of the world. He came daily to talk, and how he talked. Whether Dorothy listened or not, he kept on explaining his ideal of a world in which Christianity was not only preached but lived. He urged her to use her gift as a writer to begin a Catholic labor paper; and when she asked where the money was to come from, he answered, "God will send it." As Dorothy was to learn in the next 45 years, no matter how often her work was on the brink of folding for lack of money, God did always provide. Friends sent money and total strangers sent money, sometimes several hundred dollars for the poor, and sometimes a quarter wrapped in a bit of paper. Neither she nor the Catholic Worker movement was ever to have security; but what Peter persuaded her to begin back in 1932 never died, as its opponents prophesied it would.

They began the paper and named it the *Catholic Worker*. It was Dorothy's paper always, but Peter Maurin's "Easy Essays" set the tone and philosophy. It sold for a penny a copy. Again and again Peter, a saint-teacher and apostle to the world, told anyone who would listen that "A terrible judgment hangs over history and civilization. . . . When religion has nothing to do with education, education is only information." Dorothy said of those early days, "He made one feel the magnificent significance of our work, our daily lives, the material of God's universe, and what we did with it, how we used it, and insisted that we should be announcers, not denouncers."

What Maurin did for Dorothy was to reorient her vision; he showed her the meaning of the church and her position in it. For Dorothy, a woman of action, to know was to do. In the midst of the depression the Catholic Worker movement grew: from a paper and round-table discussions in a workers' school where priests and laymen of renown gave lectures—Father Gillis, Hilaire Belloc, Jacques Maritain, and Fathers La Farge, Furfey, and Michel—to houses of hospitality where street people might come for shelter and a bowl of soup and bread, and eventually to the farming communes (never very successful) of which Peter dreamed, where they would grow what they needed and be free of dependence on what he considered a ruthless society that preyed on its most helpless members.

It was a period of explosive activity. Young Catholics learned of the work and came to see; and some stayed to serve—a few, like young Stanley Vishnowski, for a lifetime, others for a brief but enriching period.

And although it was Peter's philosophy, it was Dorothy's practicality that gave it reality. There was no question who the leader was in the house of hospitality; and even when the idea spread to 30 other cities, one even in England, their unity of purpose was maintained by Dorothy's visits and correspondence. She was a strong woman. Some would have preferred a mellower and milder director of the work; but since she was responsible, she said, "I am not a believer in majority rule." If she was to bear the burden, hers would be the decisions. To those who would have screened their guests, she replied, "We serve the poor, worthy or unworthy." Many times over the years she herself must have found this rule of life a difficult one: not all who came were easy to get along with. Having had to fight for survival on the streets, they did not become quiet, disciplined models of propriety when they came to the houses of hospitality; nor did their language immediately soften to the dulcet tones of sobriety. But in each of these desperate faces, brutalized at times by life, Dorothy saw the suffering Christ; and if she sometimes talked them down, she seldom ordered any one out—only when obscenity and evil appeared irremediable and destructive of the community life they had established.

Dorothy Day

She was concerned about Tamar, and arranged for her to attend St. Patrick's boarding school on Staten Island. But it was evident that Tamar was not a scholar, and her interests lay in making things grow. Dorothy, torn between her obligations to her daughter, whom she loved almost fiercely, and her responsibility for the growing number of poor who came to see the houses of hospitality as home, agonized over what was best for her daughter. She enrolled her in an agricultural school in Canada, arranged for her to live and work with Ade Bethune, the artist, and wrote Tamar daily whenever they were separated—and, typically Dorothy, expected a daily card from her daughter. All the money received for the *Worker* went to pay its bills, but honoraria for articles, books and speeches Dorothy gave went for Tamar's expenses. Her father, Forster, also came to the rescue occasionally.

Father McSorley, appointed by the Archdiocese of New York as the ecclesiastical censor of the *Catholic Worker*, also became Dorothy's spiritual advisor; and he told her to accept all speaking engagements. She was not Peter Maurin—she did not enjoy lecturing others—but she accepted Father McSorley's suggestion as coming from God; and so she traveled all over the country with her single message: "We are responsible for helping our brother."

David O'Brien refers to her reiterated statement of the distinctive Worker approach: "Who are we to change anyone, and why cannot we leave them to themselves and God? What we can do is understand, love, sympathize in the sense of trying to bear a little of the suffering, and leave them—not to intrude on them

187

with the corroding pity which is often self-centered and obtuse. People must live their lives. They must bear their crosses. We have enough to do to bear our own, and how we bear our own will achieve something for those around us." But every speech carried the warning, "That extra coat in your cupboard belongs to the poor."

No matter how concrete her application of the Christian message was, her own faith grew more and more profound: almost, one might say, mystical; for it enabled her to bear the criticisms that she inevitably received. I recall hearing Dorothy speak, and her poise as barbed questions were slung at her—incredibly, it seemed to me at the time, in many cases by the clergy in the audience. I recall especially her controlled response to the question, "What are your relations with the cardinal?" She smiled and replied, "You will have to ask him what he thinks of me; I have great respect for him."

As the depression settled in, the New York house sometimes had a breadline of over 1,000; and when the donations did not match the bills, the staff would "picket St. Joseph" in the nearby church—taking turns keeping a vigil of prayer until the saint who provided for the Holy Family provided also for his foster son's needy brothers.

As she traveled more and more over the years, giving her talks, she discovered that the time became valuable for praying (she always carried a Missal, a New Testament, and her rosary), for reflection, for reading, and for writing her column for the *Worker*. There were those on the staff who sometimes criticized her, saying she accepted the speaking engagements to get away from the crowded, noisy conditions of the home. She did not bother to answer. Her life had been given to God, and she was not reneging on any part of that gift. When she was needed on the home front she was there. She participated in picketing when she felt that the laborers' cause was just. Her famous support of the cemetery workers' strike, when Cardinal Spellman refused to negotiate with them as long as their union was a CIO affiliate and called upon the seminarians to serve as grave diggers and strike-breakers, gave the movement undesirable publicity. But the archdiocese did not come off very well in that confrontation either.

She joined Cesar Chavez and his migrant workers in August, 1973, when his United Farm Workers demonstrated against the Teamsters' Union. She, together with a thousand others, was arrested and jailed for a short time. The media made much of the jailing of the frail, haggard, 76-year-old advocate of justice; and her picture on her portable chair was given publicity which gave both the grape harvesters and the *Catholic Worker* an opportunity to tell their side of the story.

Some thirty or so years earlier she had experienced the adverse effects of fighting the system. William Miller tells the story. According to Miller, "Dorothy visited the headquarters of the Southern Tenant Farmers Union in Memphis in 1936. . . . At Turrell, Arkansas, she found a company of share croppers, recently evicted from their shacks, living in tents. Half were children, and all were sick and hungry . . . a picture of dumb, helpless misery." Dorothy sent a telegram to Eleanor Roosevelt, telling her what she had witnessed.

Mrs. Roosevelt got in touch with the governor of Arkansas, who went personally to investigate. His report stated that nothing was wrong; the group was a shiftless lot who refused to work. The unfortunate publicity was the result of "a Catholic woman's action, a type that made a fat salary off the misery of the people."

The April *Worker* carried an account of the tragedy which occurred several weeks later. A group of masked riders broke into one of the tenant houses and murdered the occupant in the presence of his wife; he had witnessed the shooting of two Tenant Farmers Union organizers.

A life-long pacifist, Dorothy supported those who opposed World War II and the Vietnam war. She wrote the young men who served as conscientious objectors; and while deploring the fate of the Jews under Hitler, insisted war never solved anything. Our deploying of the atom bomb on Hiroshima and Nagasaki seemed to her an act which defied justification. The *Catholic Worker* refused to pay income taxes that would be used to buy weapons, or to participate in civil preparedness exercises. Dorothy was jailed four times between 1955 and 1960 for refusing to comply with civil defense and air raid drills, explaining to her jailers that should a bomb drop on New York, experience in Japan had proved that there would be no place to hide. Eventually the city agreed, and air raid drills were suspended.

But it was the Vietnam war which brought Dorothy one of the greatest sufferings of her life. In 1965 she had gone to Rome for ten days as a representative of the PAX group, which was asking the last session of Vatican II to issue a strong peace statement which would include conscientious objection, Gospel nonviolence, and the banning of nuclear weapons. When she returned she was faced with the tragedy of Roger La Porte, who had doused himself with gasoline in front of the United Nations building and then set himself afire, believing that his death might rouse the conscience of the world in opposition to the Vietnam war. He had never been an official member of the Catholic Worker family, but he had dropped by occasionally to help with the evening meal. As he was carried to the hospital in the ambulance he declared, "I am a Catholic Worker."

Although Dorothy did not even know the young man, and had, in fact, been in Rome when the act occurred, she and the movement came in for violent criticism, some of it by those who had been her friends and supporters. The criticism ranged from John Leo's comment that the movement had never been well-grounded intellectually to Thomas Merton's wondering whether the pacifist ideal was right when it moved a person to take his own life. Two years later Dorothy was still grieving, not only for the young life so tragically terminated but also for the unjust accusations against the movement.

When the city of New York bought some Worker property for the Verrazzano bridge, and she was able to buy a large old building on the Hudson, Dorothy began to feel less and less involved with the varied aspects of work in which the group was now engaged. In the first place she was now an old woman, and her health would not permit her to become engaged in what had been her life commitment. But she could not desert it, either. Although she loved to visit her sister Della and her husband and her daughter, Tamar, and her eight children—grandchildren whose devotion softened the last years of her life—Dorothy never stayed away from the center of things for very long.

Her last official act was when she was asked to speak at the Eucharistic Congress during the bi-centennial year. It was a moving speech, given by this frail 79-year old woman, who, together with Mother Teresa of Calcutta, illustrated for the thousands gathered there the concern and dedication of the church for the poor. But, for the thoughtful, both women stood as living conscience. They were not the church, they were members of her body; and individually and at great personal cost, both had paid the price of their living out of love of God and neighbor.

Jim Forest in his biography describes the last years. It is warming to note that, sitting by her window, she still enjoyed the beauty of the seasons, the visits of friends, and books, some of which she reread, some of which were by new authors. She had her radio and listened to the opera, watched plays and films on TV, and thought and prayed. Death had entered her life with increasing frequency, as she lost both of her parents, her brother Donald, and dear Della. Peter, of course, had gone some years before; and Peggy Baird, who joined her in becoming a Catholic; and Stanley Vishnewski; and the other Catholic Workers of the early days who now awaited her coming in heaven.

Dorothy Day

On November 29 when Tamar came to visit, Dorothy asked for a cup of tea, commented on how good small things could be, held her daughter's hand, and at 5:30 died a quiet, serene death, in striking contrast to the years of harried, tumultuous services for God's poor.

Thousands came to see her, to pray for themselves in their loss. Among them was Forster Batterham, whom Dorothy had recently visited in the hospital and whom she always referred to as her husband. She was buried on Staten Island within walking distance of the old beach house.

David O'Brien in *Commonweal* noted, "She once wrote, 'I feel that all families should have the conveniences and comforts which modern life brings, and which do simplify life, and give time to read, to study, to think and to pray. And to work in the apostolate, too. But poverty is my vocation, to live as simply and poorly as I can, and to never cease talking and writing of poverty and destitution.'" Then he adds, "But it was not Dorothy Day nor Peter Maurin, but Jesus Christ who said that the works of mercy provide the criteria of salvation. The Sermon on the Mount and not the Catholic Worker platform places the call to radical love at the heart of human history."

The question still remains to those who have the courage to ask themselves, "Why do not more of us follow it, and her?"

Simone Weil:
Enigmatic Witness to Truth

SIMONE Petrement, one of Simone Weil's personal friends and author of the biography which André Weil considers the most authentic study of his sister, states in her introduction that to present a faithful picture of her friend is a hopelessly difficult task. It would seem impossible, then, to capture this woman of contradictions in a chapter. She was a mystic (whatever that term really conveys), a highly original philosopher, a voluminous author, an uncomfortably challenging teacher. She was an activist in the French Resistance during World War II and a field and factory worker in France, and she spent a few weeks in 1936 on the front with the Republican army in Spain. A Jew by birth, a Roman Catholic by conviction, she refused on principle to be baptized. She was an intellectual whose social awareness was translated into personal action, and even today she remains an enigma to those who are attracted to her writings, as she was a paradox to those who knew and loved her during her brief life.

Simone was born on February 3, 1909, in Paris, the only daughter of free-thinking Jewish parents, and their second child. Her brother André was two years, nine months her elder. Her father, Bernard Weil, had a successful medical practice; and the children grew up in bourgeois comfort. From her eleventh to her twenty-second month she suffered from digestive difficulties; and an English pediatrician declared the baby could not live, and, if she did, she would never become a normal child.

Psychologists who read the future in an individual's early years would be gratified by hints in Simone's childhood. She was certainly not a normal child, but very soon gave indications of an extraordinary intelligence and a rare social consciousness. When she was two she heard stories about ancient Greeks and Romans from a book published by Larousse for children. One day, alone in her crib, she was heard to say, "I am afraid of the Romans." She was to reiterate this fear later in her writings on force, pointing out that the Romans' conquest of the world was built on the use of power and cruelty.

When she was three a relative gave her a ring with a small jewel. Simone refused it, saying, "I do not like luxury." That statement by a baby amused those who heard it, but it became a standard of her adult life. At five she refused sugar because the French soldiers at the front during World War I had none. A little later, when she saw poor children her age on the street with bare legs, she rolled her own warm stockings down to her ankles, since, she said, she should not have what others did not. It was a conviction that was to implement her manner of life even to the end in an English

hospital when she refused to eat more than the rations
allowed her fellow countrymen in occupied France.

Her brother André was also precocious (he later
became a brilliant mathematician); and the children
delighted in intellectual games, one of which was to
cap quotations of Racine and Corneille. Because
Simone's interests were not mathematical she was convinced she was not very gifted. As a teenager she
thought seriously about death, thinking it better to die
than to live without a motivating grasp of truth. Later
she wrote that she suddenly got the conviction that
when it is a question of spiritual gifts, he who desires
and makes every effort can finally obtain what he longs
for—"that when one hungers for bread one does not
receive stones." She added, "But at this time I had not
read the Gospels."

After finishing introductory studies at the Henry IV
Lycée, she was admitted to the Ecole Normale Supéri-
eure. There she attended Alain's philosophy classes;
and her innate feelings of revolt against the social
order, her indignation toward politicians, and her
choice of the poor as companions were reinforced. She
did not make friends easily, although hers was a sensitive and generous nature; and the friends she made
remained such during her entire life. She was shy at the
same time that she was inflexible in her beliefs. Some
of her classmates found her independent, sometimes
abrasive and almost always extreme; but Alain recognized the brilliance of his student and encouraged her
in original thinking.

It was during this time that a trait which was to

mark her for the rest of her life became obvious: she scorned style and became totally indifferent as to her appearance, dressing indifferently and devoting as little time as possible to it. Some years later, when Maurice Schumann told her that her insistence on appearing so different could be misunderstood even by her friends, she replied tearfully that she had very little energy for such things.

There is considerable truth in her explanation, for even before she entered the Normale she was plagued with migraines which left her ill and exhausted, a suffering she bore for the rest of her life. At the same time she worked, wrote and studied with feverish intensity. In an essay she wrote for Alain she says, "Sacrifice is the acceptance of pain, the refusal to obey the animal in oneself, and the will to redeem suffering men through voluntary suffering. Every saint has poured out the water; every saint has refused all well-being that would separate him from the suffering of men." It was a foreshadowing of her own life, an acceptance of pain some of her critics have considered masochistic.

Alain's comment on Simone's work at the Normale was, "Excellent student. I look forward to a brilliant success." She finished first in her class; Simone de Beauvoir ranked second that same year.

During her studies she became involved with a group of students who were known as Communists, although they never really affiliated with the party. They spent their meetings discussing Marxism and Leninism, trade unions, pacifism, war, and injustice. The papers she wrote at this time reveal original and remarkably penetrating insights into these topics, as well as colonialism, imperialism, totalitarianism, secularism, racism, and sexism. In one essay she wrote, "Culture is a privilege that gives power to the class that possesses it"—and power, she felt, was the worst of evils.

She was assigned to teach at schools in Le Puy, Auxerre, Ruanne, Bourges, and St. Quentin. Her frequent transfers arose from her difficulties with school boards and parents, seldom with students. One of the latter wrote, "The clumsiness of her gestures, above all of her hands, the special expression on her face when she would concentrate on her thought, her piercing look through her thick glasses, her smile—everything about her emanated a feeling of total frankness and forgetfulness of self, revealing a nobility of soul that was certainly at the root of the emotions she inspired in us, but that at first we were not aware of."

Simone's intense desire as a teacher was that her students should think independently. She succeeded almost too well, for, conditioned to self-expression, her students rarely did well on state examinations which traditionally expected an intellectual regurgitation of memorized material.

But it was not her style of teaching which got her into trouble with the Department of Education; it was her involvement in demonstrations, picketing with the unemployed, writing for leftist journals about the plight of the underprivileged, and refusing to eat more than those on relief. "What I cannot bear is compromise," she said to a friend. She felt strongly that there should not be the slightest discrepancy between one's beliefs and one's way of life, and joined the National

Mary Hester Valentine

Teachers Union in order to publicize her convictions to her peers.

During this period she repudiated Marx and Lenin, saying that they could not really understand the needs of the poor, especially the workers, since they had never been poor workingmen themselves. This conviction, her activities in the union, and her increased writing on the economics of power induced her to leave teaching and apply for a job in a factory.

Her unsuitability for this kind of life did not deter her. In a letter to her family she asks, "1. How do you cook rice? 2. How do you eat bacon: raw or cooked?" If you want to eat it with eggs on a plate do you have to cook it first?" Only after weeks of going without fuel did she learn that the poor did buy coal to warm their dwellings.

But it was not her ignorance of the basics of independent living on too little money which caused her the most difficulty: it was her awkwardness, and her ignorance of the demands of monotonous physical labor. She learned at personal cost the psychological effects of heavy industrial work, the pain of the "humiliated layers of the social hierarchy," as she wrote at this time. It is remarkable that she was able to write at all, for the exhausting work left her little time to formulate her conclusions. But she saw her exposé of the inhuman conditions under which factory workers toiled as important as her living with these unknown members of society. Of that year, 1934-35, she writes, "As I worked in the factory . . . the affliction of the Other entered into my flesh and my soul. Nothing separated me, for I had really forgotten the possibility of surviving all the fatigue."

Difficult as she found the deadly, dangerous monotony of the machine work, so absorbing as to numb thought, it was not this which shook her emotionally so much as the fact that she could not establish really friendly relationships with the women with whom she worked. They recognized that she was not one of them. Even though her life-style was even more frugal than theirs, they sensed it was self-chosen—although they were mystified as to why one with her obvious education and advantages should have chosen work they themselves would leave could they afford to do so.

She questioned them about their lives, but they did not tell her very much. She finally realized, as she said in her Journal, that the factory "is a jail with frantic speed-ups, a profusion of cut fingers, layoffs without the slightest twinge of conscience." She was put in a workshop where for the first time she saw a conveyer belt, which upset her very much. Working at top speed she managed to turn out 400 pieces an hour, only to be told in the late afternoon of her first day that if she did not make 800 pieces in the next two hours she could not stay on the job. She managed to hold out a month.

Someone told her that the Renault Company was hiring; and since she had learned that the man interviewing the applicants took on attractive young women, she asked a friend to make her up. With some rouge on her lips and rose-colored makeup on her cheeks she was transformed into a strikingly lovely young woman. She got the job, but after several acci-

dents and a series of fainting episodes she left the
Renault plant after a little more than two months. The
experiences were a laboratory out of which her articles on the system of economic slavery in the 20th
century were born.

After a year in the factories she went with her
parents to Portugal, admitting that the experience had
killed her youth. It was during this trip to Portugal
that she had the first of the three contacts with Catholicism "that really counted." She witnessed Portuguese wives of fishermen in their annual pilgrimage of
prayer and the blessing of the fleet, both of which
moved her internally.

Her year as a member of the industrial machine had
increased her conviction that the power exercised by
one man over another was totally dehumanizing, both
to the victim and the oppressor. The ultimate expression of this, of course, was war; and in 1936 the Spanish Civil War had erupted. Simone joined an anarchist
unit near Zaragosa, although she vowed never to carry
a gun or to shoot anyone. Because of her pacifist convictions she was assigned as assistant to the cook. To
anyone who knew her it was a ludicrous choice: her
domestic skill was limited, to say the least. Her second
day on duty she put her foot into a huge pot of boiling
oil which the cook intended to use for frying. She was
seriously burned and evacuated to a field hospital, and
later transferred to Barcelona where her parents—who
had slipped across the border—found her. After some
difficulties with the military, they succeeded in getting
her to their pensione, and, after Dr. Weil had treated

her leg, in procuring safe conduct across the border and into Paris.

The Spanish experience was for Simone a shattering one morally; and, like George Orwell, she was totally disillusioned as she saw the atrocities perpetrated by both sides. She wrote, "Our side has shed a lot of blood; morally I am an accomplice." In a letter to Georges Bernanos she explained what really changed her mind: the Spanish Civil War had become a war between Russia on the one side and Germany and Italy on the other; and the aspirations of the Spanish and Basque soldiers were overlooked by the real antagonists. In the same letter she observed that the gulf between soldiers and peasants was exactly like the gulf between rich and poor.

She had been to Germany and seen the rising anti-Semitism, and while she scorned Hitler's posturing, she saw him as a logical expression of what the entire Western world believed. In "The Need for Roots," she wrote, "Our conception of greatness is the very one that has inspired Hitler's whole life." She saw the emerging Nazi Germany as a renewal of Imperial Rome, both cultures which repressed the pursuit of freedom, dignity, beauty, and virtue. She believed that Judaism, too, was founded on power, ruthlessness, and the notion of racial superiority, and that Christianity itself had been subverted, both by its emphasis on the Old Testament and by the Roman Empire's power structure.

While recuperating from her experiences in Spain she visited Italy, an experience which was perhaps the happiest of her life. She wrote of the beauty she found here, the operas she attended, the Gregorian plainsong at St. Anselmo, and the beauty of the Pentecostal Mass at St. Peter's, adding, "There is nothing more beautiful than the texts of the Catholic liturgy." And she delighted in Italian *gelato*.

It was at Assisi that Simone had the second of the three contacts with Catholicism that she never forgot, an experience of which she spoke to her friend, Father Perrin, in 1942. "Alone, in the little 12th century Romanesque chapel of Santa Maria degli Angeli . . . something stronger than I compelled me for the first time to go down on my knees." She never revealed what this experience was in more specific terms, but the third and most enduring of her mystical experiences occurred at Solesmes during Easter of 1938. She and her mother had gone to the abbey to hear the beautiful Gregorian chants of Holy Week. They spent ten days there, from Palm Sunday to the Tuesday of Easter week. Although she was suffering from devastating headaches the entire time, she found a pure and perfect joy in the unimaginable beauty of the services, as she wrote Father Perrin. It was an experience which left her profoundly changed; she not only felt herself loved by a Superior Being, but had an understanding of divine love shining in the midst of pain. Certainly the concept of the Passion in the services affected her, but she was penetrated in a far deeper way by its personal application to her. It was an awareness which she admitted never again left her.

During this week she also came to recognize the power of the sacraments. Here, too, she was intro-

Simone Weil

duced to George Herbert's poem, "Love," which so
moved her that she later admitted that each time she
recited it she seemed to feel Christ's infinite tenderness.
She wrote of this feeling as "a presence more personal,
more certain, and more real than that of a human
person. In this sudden possession of me by Christ
neither my senses nor my imagination had any part; I
only felt in the midst of my suffering (excruciating
headaches which made doctors fear a brain tumor) the
presence of love."

(Her biographer and friend, Simone Petremont,
does not pretend to understand this. She notes that the
word "mystic" has been greatly abused, but that what
distinguishes true mystics from those who resemble
them is the quality of saintliness. A pure love, a love
that does not seek egotistical satisfactions, that seeks
the good of others—such a love can be believed when it
declares that it has encountered a supernatural reality.
The saintliness of the life is the criterion; because, if
there is saintliness it is manifested in the life, and the
reason for believing in Simone Weil's mystical experience is the evidence of her life.)

In the meantime, Hitler's "Plan" was beginning to
take shape; and the future of Europe was dark. Simone
Weil had no doubts about the impending disaster, and
she watched with horror as the German armies took
over country after country until the storm-troopers'
boots marched down the Champs Elysées. Immediately before this, however, she had participated in a
debate about Jewish immigration to Palestine—a move
she repudiated, for although she feared Arab nationalism she also feared Jewish nationalism. Her conviction

that a new state would become a tinder-box in the Middle East is almost prophetic.

As anti-Jewish laws were promulgated it became clear to Dr. and Mrs. Weil that their presence in Paris presented a very real danger; and they persuaded Simone to join them in Marseilles, then on to Vichy. During this period she helped out on farms in southern France and wrote frantically for periodicals of the Resistance. It was also during this time that her illuminating commentary on the *Illiad* appeared. It, like Jean Giraudoux's "Antigone," was written in response to the immediate tragedy of war. What Miss Weil points out in her original analysis of Homer's epic is that the heroes are the Trojan victims, although the author is Greek. He celebrates the dignity of the defeated, not the glories of the conquerors.

She was attracted to the history of religions, for in all of them she found kernels of truth—the *Epic of Gilgamesh*, the Egyptian *Book of the Dead*, the *Bhagavad Gita*, Buddhism, the Spanish mystics, Sts. Teresa and John of the Cross—and she continued to study Sanscrit and Greek, both of which she had begun as a teen-ager with her brother. Greek culture remained her favorite, although two aspects of it she chose to ignore: the fact that the Greek world rested on the solid foundation of slavery, and that only the elite "citizen" could afford to be a philosopher or artist. Aristotle's "golden mean" was at the opposite pole of her personal way of life; she was an extremist in all she did.

In 1940 she applied for a teaching post in Algeria; and when she did not receive an answer she presumed it was because of the statute concerning the employment of Jews, which had been issued on October 3. She wrote the Minister of Public Education a remarkable document in which she states she does not know the definition of the word "Jew." "Does it designate a religion? I have never entered a synagogue and I have never witnessed a Jewish religious ceremony. . . . Does this word designate a race? I have no reason to suppose that I have any relationship either through my father or my mother with the people who lived in Palestine 2,000 years ago. As far back as memory can go my father's family has lived in Alsace; my mother's family lived in a country with a Slavic population, and nothing leads me to suppose that it was composed of any group but Slavs. . . . The Christian, French, Hellenic tradition is mine; the Hebrew tradition is foreign to me, and no text of a law can change that for me." Obviously, this did not mean that Simone was explaining away her heritage out of fear, but that she was mocking the ideas on which the Anti-Semitic laws, as well as any racism, rested.

While in Marseilles she renewed her friendship with Pierre Honnorat and his sister, Helene, both of whom had also been students at the Ecole Normale. Helene was a fervent Catholic and discussed religion with Simone, who told her, "I am as close to Catholicism as it is possible to be without being a Catholic." It was through Helene that Simone met Father Perrin, to whom she wrote the famous "Letter to a Priest" which was published after her death. According to Father Perrin, "Her love of Christ seemed to be enough for her . . . however, the question of baptism came up very soon, but she explained her difficulty in becoming a

Catholic because of her admiration for the truth she saw in other religious traditions." She seems to imply that baptism might have been possible if the church were truly catholic. A friend assured her that not only those who belong to the church are saved, but also those who, outside it, are just. To her she admitted that she was possessed of a great desire to receive the Eucharist. When told one had to be in the state of grace, Simone mumbled, "I am."

She memorized the Greek text of the Our Father because, as she said, "the sweetness of the Greek text so took hold of me that for several days I could not stop myself from saying it over and over all the time." This was the first time in her life that she had formally prayed, although her experience at Solesmes was certainly a supernatural one. "Since that time," she wrote in a letter, "I have made a practice of saying it once each morning with absolute attention. If during the recitation my attention wanders, or goes to sleep in the minutest degree, I begin again until I have succeeded in going through it once with absolutely pure attention." In another place she says, "Sometimes during this recitation or at other moments, Christ is present with me in person . . . more poignant and clearer than on that first occasion when he took possession of me."

She explained to another, "What frightens me in the church is the social structure. . . . There are some saints who approved of the Crusades or the Inquisition. I cannot help thinking that they were in the wrong. I cannot go against the light of conscience."

To some this may all seem like sophism, a pride of intellect that puts itself above great minds of the ages;

but to those who knew Simone well it was obvious that she was experiencing real suffering and confusion. In Carcassone she had several interviews with a monk named Vidal who remembers, "I don't know how I came to speak of natural and Christian virtues. She asked me to list them. I cited for her as natural virtues the integrity of conscience, goodness of heart, force of will, delicacy of feelings and manners, and good manners as being the flower of charity or love. For the Christian virtues I named humility and purity. After a moment of silence she said to me very simply, 'I practice all that. And what you call grace (the supernatural help of God and a life of intimacy with him), I have this, too; I have experienced this benefit, by whatever name you wish to call it.'"

"She then told me quite definitely that Christ had possessed her one day, and had revealed himself in her, so fully did she believe in his divinity. Then she listed the problems she had which prevented her joining the church—some of which are in her 'Letter to a Priest.'"

This monk does not feel that she was kept back by intellectual pride, but that her mind could not accede blindly to truths she could not accept. To the Benedictine Don Clement Jacob she affirmed her faith in the mysteries of the Trinity, the Incarnation, and the Eucharist, but saw no possibility of ever accepting the Christian conception of history.

While in Vichy Simone became involved with the Resistance. She was suspected and summoned by the police at least twice for questioning. Her parents, in the meantime, were panic stricken each time she was arrested; and her mother remarked to a friend, "Monsieur, if you ever have a daughter, pray to God that she isn't a saint."

In the meantime the war was intensifying, and although she did not want to run away from danger Simone knew that her parents would not leave without her. Her brother was already in New York. On May 14, 1942 the Weils sailed on the steamship *Marechal-Lyautey*, transferring on June 7 to the Portuguese ship which would take them to America. The family moved into an apartment at 540 Riverside Drive in New York.

Almost immediately Simone began planning to go to England. She agonized over the thought of those wounded on the battlefields, for whom immediate care was essential. She dreamed of a small organization of nurses who would devote themselves to helping the wounded and dying in the midst of combat. She, of course, would be of that number; and she studied nursing with the Red Cross in preparation. It was totally impractical, obviously; but she seemed unaware even of the fact that her definitely Semitic features would be a danger in enemy territory not only to herself but to those with her. When the proposal was suggested to De Gaulle he snapped, "But she is mad!"

Simone wrote Jacques Maritain to try to persuade him to use his influence in getting her passage to England. She also told him of her "spiritual position," and he recommended that she get in touch with the French Dominican Father Couturier, then in the United States. She spent her time in New York studying, discussing theology and philosophy with Father Couturier and others, writing articles for the Free French in London, visiting churches, spending hours before the Blessed Sacrament, and attending Mass every Sunday.

Finally her desire to return to the scene of war became reality. She sailed on November 10, 1942, on a Swedish freighter. On board her reluctance to eat was noted, and she replied that she did not have the right to eat more than her compatriots in France. It was a conviction which was to contribute to her death.

The time in England was frustrating but mercifully short. Simone, who desired nothing so much as the opportunity to give herself to those suffering oppression, found herself caught up in the red tape of Free French officialdom in London, where she was assigned to intelligence. Although it was not the dangerous enterprise she would have chosen, she gave herself to the work with unstinting energy, sometimes staying in the office the entire night. The sheer amount of work she accomplished is staggering, and is only today being accorded its true value as a blueprint for a free world.

In a few months this pattern of overwork, joined with inadequate nourishment, took its toll; and she was hospitalized with a granular form of tuberculosis which had affected both lungs. She remained in Middlesex hospital until August 17, 1943, when she was transferred to Ashford sanitarium by ambulance. While there she cooperated with the medical staff in everything but nourishment, which by now she could not tolerate. She did try to eat liquid food—chicken broth, egg yolk with sherry—a fact which contradicts the coroner's statement that her death was suicide by starvation while the balance of her mind was disturbed. On August 24 she spoke little, fell into a coma, and died peacefully in her sleep at the age of 34, apparently of cardiac arrest. Few people twice her age have done so much under such difficulties.

In her last days she spoke often of the future, and what she would do when she could return to the continent. She wrote brief letters to her parents, sparing them the knowledge of her illness. In her last letter, however, she warned them that they might soon have a cable; it arrived before her letter. At the funeral were seven people, including her landlady.

And so her death remains a paradox, as was her life: a mystery of contradictions. Most of her writings, a total of 14 volumes, appeared posthumously, and have received the admiration Simone Weil never knew during her lifetime. She dealt with a multitude of subjects: Greek literature, her factory experiences, education, Christianity, the sacraments, grace, and always she wrote with incisiveness and a perception totally original. Lawrence Cunningham says that in her writing there is "a little something to antagonize nearly everyone," although it would not disturb Simone Weil if the reader were shocked into thinking for himself. *Time* magazine called her the saint of the churchless, the patron of the undecided, and noted that her life remains a legend encrusted in contradiction.

Was she a saint, as T. S. Eliot believed? Certainly she will not be canonized, but those who knew her and the thousands who have read her would approve what Dom Bede Griffiths says: "Of the quality of her love of neighbor and her love of God there is happily no doubt, and it is by our love that we are ultimately to be judged." Perhaps, as George Abbott White suggests in

his interpretation of her life, its meaning is simply unbearable for most of us to accept, because to do so
would require nothing less than radically changing the
meaning of our own.